THE LABOR

REFERENCE BOOK

THE
LABOR
REFERENCE
BOOK

ADRIAN A. PARADIS

CHILTON BOOK COMPANY

Philadelphia   New York   London

Library of Congress Cataloging in Publication Data

Paradis, Adrian A
    The labor reference book.

    Bibliography: p.
    1. Labor and laboring classes—United States—
Dictionaries. 2. Trade-unions—United States—
Dictionaries. I. Title.
HD8066.P37   331.1'1'0973   72-6994
    ISBN 0-8019-5727-3

1720276

With gratitude, as always,
to my wife, Grace.
Without her help none of my books
would ever be completed.

To the Reader Like its companion piece, *The Economics Reference Book,* this volume was written for the high school student and the layman who may be puzzled by the meaning or significance of various terms which he may encounter in his daily reading or study. Those seeking detailed or technical explanations of many of these terms will want to consult more advanced reference books or textbooks.

Since size limitations of the book preclude lengthy explanations of terms or long biographies of individuals, I have included only the more common words, terms, and phrases which the average student or layman might not understand. Similarly, only those historical events and labor leaders whom I consider outstanding (for one reason or another) have been mentioned. Hence the selection is by no means complete.

It is hoped, nevertheless, that enough material has been presented under each entry to enable the reader to understand what is meant by the terms or to appreciate the constructive or questionable contributions made to the labor cause by the leaders for whom brief biographies are given. Suggestions for additional reading are included in the appendix for those interested in learning more about some of the subjects.

Although the book is arranged in dictionary form, the index makes available to readers all of the information included in the numerous articles.

THE LABOR

REFERENCE BOOK

A ●●●

ALLIANCE FOR LABOR ACTION

On May 26, 1969, Walter Reuther, president of the United Auto Workers, outlined plans for a "grand alliance" to organize office workers and those industries where the AFL-CIO was only slightly represented. He also indicated that political action would be taken to change laws disliked by labor unions and to bring about various new social and economic gains for workers. Frank E. Fitzsimmons, acting chief of the Teamsters Union (while James R. Hoffa, president, was in prison on conviction of jury tampering), joined his union with Reuther's in forming the Alliance for Labor Action. This created a partnership of the nation's two largest unions, neither of which belonged to the AFL-CIO. The alliance was to be financed by a monthly assessment of ten cents on all members of each union.

Organizers for the new alliance picked Atlanta, Georgia for their first drive because this city had some 500,000 nonunion workers. During the first year a number of workers were signed up but after the death of Walter Reuther in May, 1970, progress declined and monthly dues were cut from ten cents to five cents. The drive in

Atlanta continued but most of the other activities envisioned by Reuther were not undertaken. The Alliance for Labor Action was dissolved in 1972.

AMERICAN FEDERATION OF LABOR

In 1881 trade unionists who represented some 50,000 workers founded the Federation of Organized Trades and Labor Unions of the United States and Canada (FOOTALU). Because the organization was too weak to fight the Knights of Labor which raided its membership from time to time, the new federation had difficulty in expanding. In 1885, after interunion warfare erupted among New York City cigar makers, Samuel Gompers, the head of Local 144 and an avowed enemy of the Knights, urged other trades and the FOOTALU to work for a better trade federation.

The following December, representatives of FOOTALU and several leading craft unions met in Columbus, Ohio. Taking the records and treasury of the FOOTALU, the delegates formed the American Federation of Labor (AFL) and elected Samuel Gompers president. The Knights of Labor who were then at their peak of power rejected all offers to merge the two organizations, but within fifteen years they had lost so many members that they no longer were a threat to the new AFL.

The AFL founders planned to organize workers into national unions with "strict recognition of the autonomy of each trade." The new federation consisted of independent national unions organized on the basis of crafts or trades rather than on industry. The federation would work on behalf of all the unions to improve the members' wages, hours, and working conditions, as well as to keep track of legislation. It also encouraged each union to seek collective bargaining between itself and its employers.

One of the most difficult problems the new federation faced was that of jurisdiction. If the sphere of interest of a new union was too similar to that of an affiliated member, the AFL refused it a charter and this slowed the growth of many craft unions. Those unions which were closely related were urged to merge, and many unions were encouraged to expand their jurisdictions to take in less skilled or even unskilled men. Although the federation grew, it was not long before some unions which had exclusive jurisdiction over the workers they had organized ran into trouble with the coal mining industry.

Craft unions such as boilermakers, carpenters, machinists, and patternmakers insisted that members who worked at their crafts in the coal mines should belong to the individual union which had jurisdiction over their trade. The United Mine Workers declared that it alone had jurisdiction in the mines and at its union convention held in 1901, the "Scranton Declaration" was adopted. It asserted that because coal mining was conducted away from other industries, the exclusive jurisdiction rule did not apply.

By the time World War I started, the AFL had become the accepted spokesman for the labor movement. Since the war created serious manpower shortages in many industries, the government looked with more favor upon organized labor and sought its cooperation. The National War Labor Board helped protect labor's right to organize and this added to the strength of the AFL. By 1920 the federation included more than four million members.

During the 1920's much of the new membership gained during the war was lost as the open shop returned. The depression which started in 1930 further decimated the ranks as workers lost their jobs. By 1933 the membership had declined to 2,127,000, consisting mostly of coal miners, railroad shop craftsmen, and building trades workers.

Meanwhile, William Green became AFL president in 1924 upon the death of Samuel Gompers.

Although the New Deal was friendly to labor and helped guarantee a union's right to organize and bargain collectively, the AFL suffered a serious reversal after John L. Lewis and others in the federation insisted that mass production industries like automobiles, rubber, or steel, be organized on an industrial basis rather than as crafts. The proposal for industrial unionism was roundly defeated by the members in 1935, whereupon eight unions set up the Committee for Industrial Organization within the AFL. Under Lewis' leadership the new CIO commenced to organize unions in steel, glass, rubber, automobiles, and other industries and by the end of 1937 had signed up 3,700,000 members compared with the AFL's 3,400,000. All members of the CIO were thereupon expelled from the AFL, and in 1938 the CIO changed its name to Congress of Industrial Organizations. As a result of this breach, the AFL switched its policy regarding exclusive jurisdiction in manufacturing industries. Then its organizers went out and won more new members than those recruiting for the CIO.

Following World War II rivalry continued between the two unions, although from time to time committees were formed to effect a reconciliation. The attitude of older labor leaders who were bitter at Lewis and the others who had broken away, and the fact that Communists dominated some of the CIO unions kept the two groups apart. The eventual disappearance of the oldtimers, the ousting of the Communists, the election of George Meany in 1953 to replace William Green, and the signing of a no-raiding agreement that same year by both unions led to an official merger into the AFL-CIO in December, 1955. George Meany, who had worked hard to effect the merger, was elected the first president of the new union. The only subsequent serious break in the ranks occurred in 1968 when Walter Reuther established the United Automobile Workers as an independent union.*

Today all of the affiliated unions send representatives to the AFL-CIO convention which is held every other year. The convention elects the officers, including twenty seven vice presidents who make up the executive council. This group carries out policies, handles legislative matters, and administers the organization's affairs between conventions. Fourteen committees deal with a wide range of activities such as civil rights, education, housing, legislation, public relations, research, etc. Political activities are undertaken by national and local Committees on Political Education (COPE) which was established to help elect legislators friendly to the AFL-CIO.

The AFL-CIO has approximately 125 national and international individual and trade unions, a membership of some fifteen million. The national unions have local affiliates in the United States and its territories, while the international unions have signed up affiliates in Canada, Mexico, Panama, and Puerto Rico. More than sixty thousand locals belong to the national and international unions.

(See also: Congress of Industrial Organizations; Samuel Gompers; William Green; John L. Lewis; George Meany; Walter Reuther.)

AMERICAN LABOR PARTY

". . . it is obvious to industrial workers that the labor movement must organize and exert itself not only in the

---

* In 1957 the Teamsters Union, Laundry Workers, and Bakers Union were expelled as a result of the McClellan Committee hearings.

American Liberty League

economic field but also in the political arena. . . ." John
L. Lewis wrote in the mid-thirties.

To carry out this idea the CIO established the Non-
Partisan League in 1936 and at the same time was helpful
in forming the American Labor Party in New York. The
purpose of both organizations was to assure the re-election
of President Franklin D. Roosevelt. Every effort was made
to gain support of the membership of both the AFL and
CIO unions.

The Communists gained control of the American Labor
Party during the 1940's. The Party opposed the Truman
administration and in the 1948 election supported Henry
A. Wallace, the Progressive Party candidate. Thereafter it
had little effect on the national political scene and disappeared by the middle 1950's.

AMERICAN LIBERTY LEAGUE

This was a political organization formed during the
early 1930's by business and financial leaders who opposed
the policies of President Franklin D. Roosevelt. Their
purpose was to "combat radicalism, protect property
rights and to uphold and preserve the Constitution." The
league sponsored numerous radio programs and published
pamphlets to rally public opinion against the New Deal.

As soon as the Wagner Act was adopted on July 5, 1935,
Earl F. Reed, counsel to the Weirton Steel Company and
chairman of the league's legal committee, stated that he
considered the act unconstitutional and would advise his
clients not to feel bound by law. This advice proved erroneous and the membership soon lost interest in the league
after it failed to win support in the 1936 presidential election.

6

AMERICAN PLAN

During the early 1920's business leaders were anxious to curb the strength which unions had gained during World War I. They backed an anti-union campaign aimed at maintaining the open shop, an arrangement which meant that an employer was free to hire any workers he chose regardless of whether or not they belonged to a union. In practice, managements usually discriminated against hiring union members. More important, however, a group of workers was usually unable to force its employer to engage in collective bargaining because no union represented them.

State employer groups helped organize open shop associations throughout the country and gave this principle the patriotic name "American Plan." At the same time businessmen, chambers of commerce, manufacturers' associations, the National Association of Manufacturers, the National Metal Trades Association, and other business organizations supported the movement.

The idea caught on quickly. Bethlehem Steel Corporation not only adopted the open shop policy but refused to sell steel to those builders who refused to do the same. Meat packers in Chicago cancelled their union agreements in favor of open shops. Building trade unions, textile unions, and some of the newer unions founded during the war suddenly were forced to contend with the open shop. In 1922 a railroad strike ended with the open shop fairly well entrenched (this was reversed in 1926 when the Railway Labor Act provided for the formation of unions in the industry), and gradually "yellow-dog" contracts returned along with company unions, company labor spies, and company police patrolling many plants.

Collective bargaining was replaced in most companies

by labor-management cooperation which, where it existed, depended upon an employer's good will for any extra benefits he might give his employees. The situation did not change until 1933 when Section 7(a) of the National Labor Relations Act guaranteed employees the right to organize and bargain collectively.
(See also: Antiunion Campaigns; Collective Bargaining; National Industrial Relations Act.)

ANARCHO-SYNDICALISM

The wave of immigrants which flooded into America after the Civil War included some radicals who were eager to indoctrinate labor with the anarchistic ideas then prevalent in Europe. Anarchists believed that government was not compatible with individual and social liberty and therefore it should be abolished. In place of government they wanted to substitute voluntary cooperation and mutual assistance. In order to gain their objectives they advocated general strikes, terror, lawless confusion, and political disorder. Once they had won control of the populace, they would institute syndicalism. This meant that groups of workers would take over all factories and industries, oust the owners, and operate the businesses.

The American branch of the revolutionary International Workingmen's Association * had been dissolved in 1876 and Socialist sympathizers formed a new Working Men's Party. The membership was insignificant, but during the railway strike of 1877, its leaders tried to start a

* In 1864 the International Workingmen's Association was organized at Saint Martin's Hall, London, under Karl Marx's auspices. To thwart anarchistic forces which tried to gain control of the Association, the Socialists, who controlled the membership, moved the organization's headquarters to New York where it eventually died and with it Marx's hopes for using trade unions to attain a socialistic state.

general strike and instigate violence. Disputes soon split the party's ranks and the revolutionist element rallied around Johann Most, a huge black-bearded immigrant who had arrived from Germany in 1882. He believed in revolutionary violence and helped organize the Working People's Association (better known as the Black International) which soon won control of the Central Labor Union in Chicago. Although the membership of the Chicago group probably never exceeded two thousand, the newspapers emphasized its dangerous nature. After the Haymarket Square Riot, which the Black International helped foment, the influence of anarchists on the trade union movement quickly diminished.

(See also: Haymarket Riot.)

ANTIUNION CAMPAIGNS

Historically and traditionally employers have been staunchly opposed to any unionization move on the part of their employees. In the 1830's they expressed regret at "the formation of any society that has a tendency to subvert good order, and coerce or molest those who have been industriously pursuing their avocation and honestly maintaining their families." This philosophy had been supported by the courts which held that common law prohibited combinations and conspiracy in restraint of trade, and therefore strikes and labor unions were both illegal. The natural laws of supply and demand were the only legal ruling forces and should be allowed to take care of all such problems.

Actually the purpose of the early employer associations was to destroy the unions which employers claimed encouraged "oppression, tyranny, and misrule" and blocked "the free course of trade." The new factories found the blacklist their most effective weapon at this time.

9

Antiunion Campaigns

It was not until 1842 that a Massachusetts judge decided in the case of *Commonwealth v. Hunt* that unions were not guilty of conspiracy in restraint of trade and that it was not illegal for a union to strike for higher wages. The workingman had his first great victory, but the fact that he was free to organize and strike did not mean that right would win over might.

During the Civil War unionism grew so rapidly that many employers formed their own organizations to repress labor unions. Antilabor legislation appeared in the states, and as soon as the war was over and a postwar recession with widespread unemployment had begun, employers set out to crush one local after another by using the "yellow-dog" contract, the blacklist, the lockout, and other weapons.

Many of the employers' associations were local groups concerned with a single trade but there were also city federations and regional groups. One national organization, the American National Steel Manufacturers' and Iron Founders' Association, was also actively working for anti-labor legislation.

Industrialism grew rapidly once the nation recovered from the postwar depression. The labor movement made gains but the country was torn from time to time for the next forty years by almost continuous labor turmoil. Although the Knights of Labor prospered, the lot of the workingman did not greatly improve. Many of the strikes were failures, and once a strike was called off the union members were usually blacklisted, unable to obtain work, and replaced by strikebreakers. The Molly Maguire Riots of 1875, the destructive railroad strike of 1877, and the Haymarket Riot of 1886, plus other labor disputes all gave labor a bad reputation.

Many people had the impression that workingmen were criminals who wanted to steal, kill, riot, burn property, and overthrow the existing order. Waves of strikes and the emergence in labor circles of a new anarchist element bent on revolutionary violence created antiunion campaigns. Courts prosecuted union members for rioting and conspiracy, and state legislatures passed laws that curbed the activities of labor unions.

Following the depression of 1893, an increasing labor supply was needed as factories became busy again. When workers returned to their jobs, many joined unions and the AFL's membership grew. This trend alarmed the employers who again responded with their employers' associations. In 1901 the Dayton Employers Association was founded to wage a campaign against union labor. Employer members were pledged to fight for the open shop; to achieve their goal they hired nonunion workers, organized strikebreaking agencies, used spies in their plants, and, when necessary, closed down factories for a week or two so that they could rehire only nonunion help. This association served as a model for other cities where similar groups of employers attacked the open shop. Meanwhile the National Association of Manufacturers led a movement to oppose further recognition of unions, and the Citizens' Industrial Association conducted an educational program that labeled the closed shop as "un-American." As a result AFL affiliates lost many of their strikes and the labor movement suffered a setback until the outbreak of World War I.

With the declaration of war between the United States and Germany in 1917, labor pledged to aid the war effort, and in return for certain promises President Wilson's administration granted labor most of the rights it had been

11

demanding for so many years: the right to organize and bargain collectively, equal pay for equal work, the eight-hour day as far as possible, and the right of all to a living wage.

Although during the war capital and labor observed a temporary truce, it was soon to end. Many corporations quickly showed a disposition to break any trust the workingmen might have placed in them and to run roughshod over labor whenever it suited their best interests. Another antiunion campaign aimed at maintaining the open shop appeared under the name of the "American Plan," and collective bargaining disappeared in most plants until 1933 when the National Labor Relations Act guaranteed employees the right to organize and bargain collectively.

During World War II, mostly as a result of the strikes by John L. Lewis' United Mine Workers union, five states passed laws prohibiting the closed shop or union security agreements and Congress adopted the Smith-Connally bill in 1943. This legislation permitted strikes only after a strike vote was taken by the National Labor Relations Board during a thirty-day "cooling-off" period, and provided that any factory could be seized if a strike threatened the war effort. It also stipulated criminal penalties for individuals who advocated a strike, and forbade union contributions to political campaigns. Although President Roosevelt vetoed the bill the Congress enacted it over his veto.

All was not going against labor, however. The Supreme Court was supporting the National Labor Relations Board by handing down decisions favorable to the workingman, affirming his right to strike, to picket, and to conduct boycotts. In *Thornhill v. Alabama* peaceful picketing was declared a legitimate exercise of free speech. In

Hunt v. Cromboch which involved the Sherman Act and was decided in 1945, the court upheld the right of a union to conduct boycotts that could practically force a company out of business.

Following World War II numerous, widespread, and often crippling strikes, drives for higher wages, and the frightening power of John L. Lewis and some other labor leaders aroused many congressmen. In 1946 the lawmakers passed the Lea Act which curbed the activities of James C. Petrillo, president of the American Federation of Musicians. The Case bill, passed by both the House and Senate during the railroad strike of May 1946 would have curbed labor unions severely but President Harry Truman vetoed it. The following year Congress passed the Taft-Hartley Act over the President's veto. During this same period many states passed antiunion laws, sixteen of them prohibiting the closed shop, twenty-one requiring strike notices and cooling-off periods, eleven restricting picketing, twelve forbidding secondary boycotts. Ten forced unions to file financial reports, and six removed prohibitions against the use of injunctions in labor disputes.

In spite of these restrictions, labor unions managed to increase their membership from fifteen million in 1950 to over twenty million in 1971. During the 1960's many unions were forced to defend themselves against charges of union corruption, union monopoly, featherbedding, and excessive power. If further antiunion campaigns are to come from employers, the focus will very likely be concentrated on the issue of union monopoly.

(See also: American Plan; Haymarket Riot; Industrial Alliances; Molly Maguire Riots; National Labor Relations Act; Strikes; Taft-Hartley Act; Union Monopoly.)

13

Apprenticeship

APPRENTICESHIP

This term refers to a period of service when a worker is trained in a skilled trade under the instruction of a company or a master.

The apprenticeship system had its origin in medieval Europe. Guilds and corporations controlled the economic life of the feudal society through monopolistic charters granted them by kings, princes, barons, and other rulers. The highest standards of workmanship were insisted upon, and those who wished to qualify for employment had to gain practical experience under a master's direction for a seven year period.

The apprenticeship system spread to England and eventually to the American colonies. Prior to the Revolutionary War many boys were apprenticed by their parents to men who were legally known as masters. The youths usually lived with the masters, were required to obey them, and to work for them for the usual seven year period. One of the best known apprentices was Benjamin Franklin who learned the printing trade in his brother's shop. By the 1800's the apprenticeship system had almost disappeared.

It was not until the early 1900's that Wisconsin established a state system of apprenticeships. This proved so successful that Congress adopted the Apprentice-Training Service Act in 1937. With this encouragement many states now sponsor apprentice programs which give those learning a trade the opportunity to earn while they work. Some of the trades open to apprenticeship include those of house painter, tailor, carpenter, plumber, electrician, and upholsterer.

To become an apprentice one must be between sixteen and twenty-four years old and a high school graduate. An apprentice agrees to work and also attend classroom instruction for two or more years. His rate of pay increases during this time but averages about fifty per cent of the regular wage paid a skilled journeyman. Once an apprentice has completed his training and indicates ability to practice his craft, he can seek employment and is known as a *journeyman*.

Minorities have experienced difficulty gaining acceptance into the skilled trades, particularly in the construction industry. In many cities Joint Apprenticeship Programs have been established to assist black youths who wish to enter apprenticeship training courses of the various building crafts unions. Other apprenticeship programs are available from time to time and the United States Training and Employment Service administers a network of thirty-six Apprenticeship Information Centers in twenty-three states and the District of Columbia. At each of these centers potential applicants are recruited, interviewed, tested, counseled, and referred to apprenticeship career opportunities where special emphasis is placed on serving minority groups whenever possible.

Apprenticeship is again on the decline because machines and mass production methods are doing much of the work formerly performed by artisans. Furthermore the greater availability of technical and vocational education makes it possible to learn a well-paying trade in a shorter time than the usual apprentice period.

ARBITRATION

When two parties are unable to agree on how to solve a problem, they submit their differences to a third party, or arbitrator, and agree to be bound by his decision. This is known as arbitration. Usually each party decides which issues the arbitrator will decide. In voluntary arbitration labor and management agree to submit their differences to an arbitrator and obey his decision, but in compulsory arbitration a governmental body orders that a dispute must be decided by arbitration because the matter is so important that it affects the public interest.

Most collective bargaining agreements include a clause which stipulates that if the employer and union cannot agree in a labor grievance or dispute, they will submit the matter to arbitration. If an arbitrator is appointed to hear just one case it is called temporary or ad hoc arbitration. However, if the same individual conducts all of the arbitrations that may come up after a contract has been signed, it is known as permanent arbitration.

The decision of the arbitrator, known as the award, is usually written and generally follows an opinion giving the reasons for the decision. The award is binding on both parties but in most states it is possible to appeal such a decision to the courts if the award was obtained by corruption or fraud, if the arbitrator exceeded his authority, was prejudiced or corrupt, or if either of the parties did not have a fair hearing.

In 1886 the federal government passed a voluntary arbitration law which applied only to railroads and other transportation companies engaged in interstate commerce. That same year Massachusetts and New York enacted statutes providing for permanent arbitration boards which could be called upon by management or labor to hear any dispute.

Following World War I the Kansas legislature enacted a law which called for compulsory arbitration. It prohibited strikes in industries which involved the public interest and ruled that all such disputes must be submitted to arbitration. In 1922 the U.S. Supreme Court in *Wolff*

Packing Co. v. Court of Industrial Relations weakened the law by declaring that compulsory arbitration in the meat packing industry was unconstitutional.

Most labor unions have accepted arbitration as the final step in plant grievance procedures, but they rarely agree to it when they have reached an impasse in bargaining for wages, hours of labor, better working conditions, fringe benefits, etc. Many union leaders fear that their position of leadership is threatened if important issues are settled in this manner rather than by calling for a strike.

"We are getting to the point where a strike doesn't make sense in many situations," George Meany, president of the AFL-CIO said in 1970. "We find that, more and more, strikes don't settle a thing." Although insisting that workers must have the right to strike, he admitted that voluntary arbitration rather than the compulsory arbitration forced on each party in a dispute might be an effective substitute for strikes. Subsequently representatives of the American Arbitration Association, labor unions, and business met to weigh arbitration as a strike alternative.

The American Arbitration Association, founded in 1926, offers the services of some 21,000 men and women who are skilled arbitrators. They operate under established procedural rules and help settle commercial, labor, international trade, and accident disputes.

ASSOCIATIONISTS

Associationists or American Fourierists spearheaded a movement which was based on the teachings of the French social economist, Charles Fourier (1772–1837). According to Fourier, our social order is based on fixed intellectual and moral laws which man must discover for himself and obey. Therefore society must be so arranged that each man may be free to indulge his own wishes. Industry, he felt, must be carried on by elaborate socioeconomic organizations which he called phalanxes.

Leaders of the Associationists, including Horace Greeley, the famous newspaper editor and politician, believed that employers and employees shared a common interest. These Fourierists advocated phalanxes, community life, and the ten-hour day. The evils of the new industrialism disturbed them, and to escape the sordid factory life of that day they purchased Brook Farm.*

The Associationists did not believe in strikes. They held there was a better chance that the employer would voluntarily improve the worker's lot if employees did not band together. The workingmen's associations obviously opposed the Associationists and the movement died out by the early 1840's.

AUTOMATION

Very simply stated, automation is one or more machines that can control themselves. Automation exists when machines are controlled by other machines or devices instead of by men. An automated system must be able to make choices, operate after it has made a choice, and then control its own activities. One definition says that automation is "the application of feedback principles, whereby a mechanical system automatically observes and regulates its own performance, thus eliminating the need for human control."

An important characteristic of automation is the feed-

---

* A community established in 1841 near West Roxbury, Massachusetts where everyone shared in the work and received equal pay. The community was successful until fire destroyed the main building in 1846 after which the project was dissolved.

back process. Because a machine has ability to send back instructions to itself, it can control and correct what it is doing and thus avoid mistakes or disaster. The familiar thermostat found in most homes is a typical feedback protective device. Its function is to keep the house at the temperature you have selected. As soon as the thermostat registers a drop in temperature it switches on electric current which starts the furnace. Once the proper temperature has been reached the thermostat sends back another signal to stop the furnace and prevent the house from overheating.

Another term, cybernation, was invented by Dr. Norbert Wiener (1894–1964), a world-famous scientist, often called the father of automation. Cybernation is the operation of a machine by a computer. The computer does the "thinking" and gives instructions to the machine which then performs certain tasks as directed by the computer.

The dial telephone is an example of cybernation. As you dial, the instrument sends instructions to the central switching machine. This apparatus searches for the number you want and as soon as it has found it, rings the bell on the other end. Machines hooked up to computers are being used to do a wide variety of tasks and no one knows, of course, what computers will be able to do in the future.

Automation reduces the number of jobs because it eliminates the need for many workers who formerly tended machines. Government, management, and unions have worked together to protect workers affected by automation. Shorter workdays or workweeks, extra holidays, longer vacations, job guarantees, and early retirement are some of the ways jobs have been protected.

The Manpower Development and Training Act of 1962 and the Economic Opportunity Act of 1964 offered training programs to give those workers unemployed by automation the opportunity to learn different crafts. Such programs are meaningless, however, unless jobs exist for the workers who have acquired new skills.

The dehumanizing effects of automation have been known and argued for sometime, but it was not until early in 1972 when workers at the General Motors' Lordstown, Ohio, plant walked out that management was forced to face the problem realistically. At the struck factory, which was built to produce a hundred Vegas an hour to meet West German and Japanese competition, labor turmoil had grown to the explosion point in spite of good wages and benefits within the plant and a high national unemployment rate outside. The employees, whose average age was under twenty-five, made no secret of their bitterness as had increasing numbers of workers in other mass production industries.

The real question was this: how could heightened productivity (which is the key to protecting jobs, paying high wages, and guaranteeing good fringe benefits) be adjusted to and reconciled with the need to preserve the individual worker's sense of worth and his mental and physical well being? It appeared that the answer would call for long hours at the bargaining table and basic changes in many of our robot ruled factories.

B ●●

"BATTLE OF THE OVERPASS"

On May 26, 1937, a group of CIO union organizers, including Walter Reuther and Richard Frankensteen, approached an overpass to the Ford Motor Company plant prepared to pass out literature to employees. Henry Ford was adamant that he would never recognize a union, and his police (referred to as service men) ordered the CIO men to leave. In the ensuing scuffle, "The Battle of the Overpass," one of the organizers was savagely beaten. Later he testified:

"They picked me up about eight different times and threw me down on my back on the concrete. While I was on the ground they kicked me in the face, head, and other parts of my body . . . I never raised a hand. After they kicked me down all the stairs then they started to hit me at the bottom of the stairs, hit me and slugged, driving me before them, but never letting me get away."

Four years later Ford was ordered by the Supreme Court to obey the 1938 findings of the National Labor Relations Board. The company had to rehire and pay two million dollars in back wages to the 2,566 workers who the Labor Board ruled had been discharged illegally for union membership. A week later company bulletin boards displayed notices stating that employees were free to organize if they wished and shortly thereafter Ford signed a contract with the United Automobile Workers.

(See also: Richard Frankensteen; Walter Reuther.)

BECK, DAVID

This labor leader was born in Stockton, California, on June 16, 1894. He was educated in the Seattle public schools and took extension courses at the University of Washington.

Early in his career Dave Beck became involved in union activities and was appointed a part-time organizer for the International Brotherhood of Teamsters, Chauffeurs, Warehousemen and Helpers of America in 1925, a general organizer in 1927, then a vice-president, executive vice-president, and president. Beck believed in "business unionism"—that labor unions are another form of business and should be run as such. During the early 1930's he built the Teamsters Union into one of the strongest in the country and from the mid-1930's until the mid-1950's wielded considerable economic and political power in the city of Seattle.

Dave Beck was one of the best known labor leaders to come out in support of Dwight D. Eisenhower's two election campaigns. In 1957, however, Senator John L. McClellan embarrassed the administration when he charged that Beck had misappropriated hundreds of thousands of dollars of union funds and had also accepted "loans" from employers. By this time Beck was a vice-president of the AFL-CIO as well as president of the Teamsters.

The hearings brought out accusations that he had borrowed money from companies which employed union members, had connections with west coast racketeers, had engaged in acts of violence and terrorism, and had misappropriated union funds. Senator McClellan denounced Beck and James Hoffa, another Teamsters' executive, as leaders of a "racket-ridden, gangster infested, and scandal packed" union. In 1958 Beck was sentenced to prison on charges of income tax evasion and larceny, and at the same time the Teamsters Union was expelled from the AFL-CIO. As a result of this incident, the Ethical Practices Committee of the AFL-CIO urged adoption of a law that would control management of union pension and welfare funds. The next year Congress passed the Landrum-Griffin Act which erected safeguards against irresponsible and corrupt union leadership.

BERGER, VICTOR LOUIS

This early Socialist was born in Nieder Rehbach, Austria-Hungary, on February 28, 1860. After receiving his education in Vienna and Budapest, he emigrated to the United States in 1878 and settled in Milwaukee where he taught school and became active in various Socialist groups. In 1892 he founded and became editor of the *Wisconsin Vorwärts* which he edited until 1898. Later, from 1901–1911, he edited the *Social Democratic Herald,* a weekly newspaper, and its successor, the daily *Milwaukee Leader,* until his death in 1929.

Joining forces with Eugene V. Debs and others, he helped form the Social Democratic Party which later became the Socialist Party. Berger became the first Socialist to be elected to the House of Representatives (1911–1913). Here he worked hard for social legislation which included child labor laws, the eight-hour day, federal relief for farmers, and old-age pensions. Following this initial term, he was not elected again until 1918 but was refused his seat because he had taken an anti-war position during World War I. Indicted and convicted under the Espionage Act of 1917 because of his unpatriotic stand, Berger was sentenced to twenty years in prison but on appeal to a higher court was released. His constituents voted for him again in 1919, but he was not admitted to the Congress until the United States Supreme Court reversed his conviction in 1921. He then served continuously till his death on August 7, 1929.

Berger was an idealist who spoke out fearlessly for the principles of his party. His lifetime goal was to build a socialist society by using the ballot and adopting social reforms through established legal means rather than by resorting to violence.

BESPOKE WORK

During the colonial period many master workmen had their own shops where they employed journeymen and apprentices. The orders which came into such shops for handmade articles were known as "bespoke work."

BLACKLIST

This term refers to a list of people who are suspected of having done something wrong or thought to deserve blame or punishment for what they may have done.

Companies have used blacklists as a weapon to fight unions. This was especially true during the period of 1870–1890. Employers circulated lists of employees who were suspected of belonging to unions or who held beliefs which the management considered undesirable or dangerous. Labor unions blacklisted employers by exchanging lists of companies which treated employees unfairly or had antiunion policies. Unions also recorded the names of employees who refused to join a union or acted as strikebreakers.

It is illegal to compile blacklists in most states, and the Federal Fair Labor Standards Act of 1938 outlawed this practice.

BOSTON POLICE STRIKE

On September 9, 1919 at 5:45 p.m., 1,117 of the Boston police force of 1,544 men walked off their beats after some two dozen patrolmen had been suspended for joining the new AFL union. Reports of what happened are conflicting, but apparently the state guard and volunteer police who were ready to patrol the city were purposely withheld so that lawlessness would occur and further incense the public against the striking policemen.

Mobs smashed some windows and looted some stores, whereupon the mayor called in the militia to restore order and guard the city. After Police Commissioner Edwin U. Curtis fired the men he had previously suspended, Samuel Gompers, president of the AFL, sent a telegram to then Governor Calvin Coolidge complaining that the action was unwarranted. The governor's often quoted reply was that there was "no right to strike against the public safety by anybody, anywhere, anytime." Coolidge became a national hero and there was general agreement that policemen were not justified to use the strike as a weapon.

The belief that public workers could not strike changed drastically during the 1960's when groups of unionized public employees began widespread strikes to win their demands.

In 1947 the New York State Legislature passed the controversial Condon-Wadlin Act following a teachers' walkout in Buffalo. The revolutionary legislation prohibited strikes by public employees and required all guilty employees be dismissed. Should strikers be rehired, they had to remain on probation for five years and could receive no pay increases for three years. The penalties were so severe that the law was rarely invoked and after twenty years was replaced by the milder Taylor Act in April, 1967. This statute guaranteed unions the right to organize and bargain for public employees, established a Public Employment Relations Board to provide mediation and arbitration services, barred strikes, provided stiff fines for unions which struck, and deprived striking unions of dues-checkoff * privileges for a maximum of eighteen months.

The Taylor Act was not uniformly enforced. Some unions were allowed to strike without receiving penalties, while others were fined and their leaders imprisoned. Albert Shanker, president of New York City's United Federation of Teachers, made no attempt to avoid jail when he and his union defied the law in 1967 and 1968.

In 1972 the Workers Defense League, a labor-rights organization founded in 1937, sponsored a meeting to discuss the no-strike ban placed on public employees. The league had been opposed to jailing labor leaders following strikes by employees. Union leaders and Theodore W. Kheel, a well known attorney and labor mediator, spoke out against the Taylor Act.

"Compulsory arbitration, labor courts, the Taylor Act, fact-finding, won't work," Mr. Kheel said. "The only way to achieve true collective bargaining, there is no other way, is to include provisions for the right to strike and the right to take a strike vote." Others insisted that public employees had as much right as other workers to strike and asserted that laws and injunctions used by government to prevent strikes were really attempts to destroy unions.

* Under the checkoff system workers authorize their employer to collect their union dues or deduct them from their paychecks and give the money to the union.

BOUND LABOR

During colonial times many British workingmen who wanted to live in the American colonies bound themselves out as indentured servants. They did this by signing contracts with merchants who agreed to hire them. The unsuspecting laborers were led to believe that their future employers would advance the cost of their passage, and that they would quickly be able to earn it back and then be free to work wherever they wished. Upon arrival in America they discovered that the required length of service was one to seven years, averaging usually at four. Sometimes the immigrants also had to agree to pay for the passage of those who had died en route.

A typical advertisement might read: "Just arrived from London . . . a parcel of young likely men-servants consisting of Weavers, Joyners, Shoemakers, Smiths . . . and several other trades, and are to be sold very reasonable either for ready money, Wheat, Bread or Flour by Edward Hoane in Philadelphia."

Some of the indentured servants had been sentenced to labor because of minor offenses committed in the mother country, but many had been kidnapped, especially children. It was estimated that half of the immigrants who came to colonial America were indentured servants and that by 1770 some 250,000 had immigrated, 100,000 of whom were victims of kidnapping or prisoners sent to serve their sentences in the colonies.

BOYCOTT

This term refers to the refusal of an individual or a group to do business with or have anything to do with another person, company, organization, or country.

Captain Charles Boycott, a British merchant who lived

27

in Ireland during the Land League agitation in 1880, was responsible for the term. He was so cruel to the Irish tenants of his employer, Lord Erne, that his neighbors would neither buy from nor sell to him. The word is now used to refer to action taken by a labor union against an unfair employer. A primary boycott is the refusal of union members to do business with their employer. A secondary boycott exists when a union influences or persuades others to join in the action. Boycotts are one of the weapons used by unions to strike back at employers during a labor-management dispute.

The Taft-Hartley Act, as amended in 1959, prohibits secondary boycotts. Some state statutes forbid all boycotts because they are interpreted as being in restraint of trade.

Minority groups have used the boycott successfully, especially in fighting for civil rights. In 1956 southern blacks boycotted the bus companies that segregated their passengers. In other instances minorities have successfully used the boycott against businesses which discriminated in their hiring practices.

BRANDEIS, LOUIS DEMBITZ

This famous American jurist was born in Louisville, Kentucky on November 13, 1856. Following graduation from Harvard Law School in 1877, he practiced law in Boston until 1916. He quickly became known as the "People's attorney" because he served many Bostonians without pay. Among other actions, he fought to control the price of gas and represented policyholders when he investigated life insurance companies and prepared state legislation to control them. He opposed the New Haven Railroad's transportation monopoly in New England and worked against other economic and power groups.

In addition to his work in Boston, Brandeis also acted

as "counsel for the people" in numerous legal actions, including those which involved the minimum wage law in Oregon, California's eight-hour law, and the women's ten-hour laws in Illinois and Oregon. In 1916 President Woodrow Wilson nominated Brandeis an associate justice of the Supreme Court.

Justice Brandeis was generally in favor of the New Deal legislation but voted against the National Industrial Recovery Act in 1935. He resigned in 1939 and devoted himself to Zionist affairs until his death in Washington, D.C. on October 5, 1941.

BRIDGES, HARRY

Harry Bridges (Alfred Renton Bridges) was born in Melbourne, Australia on July 28, 1901. He came to the United States as a seaman in 1920 and joined the International Longshoremen's Association (ILA). During 1934 he led the widespread west coast maritime strike and in 1937 left the ILA and set up the International Longshoremen's and Warehousemen's Union (ILWU) of which he became president. This union was later expelled from the CIO because it was Communist dominated.

Bridges affirmed his sympathy with Communism but denied that he was ever a party member. On several occasions the government tried to revoke his citizenship and deport him. In 1960 the ILWU signed the first labor agreement to contain provisions dealing with automation. More recently, in 1971–72, Bridges led his union in a strike which tied up the entire west coast waterfront for several weeks.

BROTHERHOOD

An association of men who band together for some purpose. Many groups of workers who have organized unions

use the word "brotherhood" in the name of their society
to imply a fraternal purpose to their venture.

C ••

CHECKOFF

When employees authorize their employer to deduct
their union dues from their paychecks and give the money
to their union it is referred to as the "checkoff."

CHILD LABOR

The U.S. Department of Labor defines child labor as
the employment of girls and boys who are too young to
work for hire, or who are employed at jobs unsafe or un-
suitable for children their age or at occupations which are
harmful to their welfare.

In the latter 1770's when the factory system was introduced in England, young children were exploited by the
owners. Children worked for lower wages than adults,
their small fingers could reach into and fix machines
quickly, and they rarely caused labor problems. This was
also true in the United States; child labor continued until
the end of the 19th century when children eight and ten
years old still took care of cotton looms in some factories,
and boys slightly older worked in factories and mines,
often tending dangerous machines.

From time to time social workers called attention to the

shameful way children were being exploited in many places and were successful in getting remedial legislation passed in some states. Massachusetts enacted the first child labor law in 1836, setting the minimun age of fifteen for employment of children in factories. Even fifteen-year-olds could be hired only if they had attended school the previous year for at least three months. In many parts of the country, however, lawmakers resisted attempts to abolish child labor because they were anxious to have this cheap labor force to attract new industry.

In 1909 President Theodore Roosevelt called the first White House Conference on Children to consider child welfare problems. As a result of this meeting the U.S. Children's Bureau was established that same year to be a research and educational agency.

In 1916 Congress passed the Child Labor Act (also known as the Owen-Keatings Bill) which forbade interstate shipments of products made by child labor, but the law was declared unconstitutional in 1918 by the Supreme Court. The lawmakers tried again in 1919 by basing the legislation on Congress' taxing authority but this bill was voided also. A constitutional amendment adopted by Congress to regulate the labor of young people under eighteen failed to gain the necessary approval of two-thirds of the states. Late, in 1933, child labor was regulated by the National Industrial Recovery Act. Although the entire law was declared invalid in 1935, the public at that time had accepted the idea of regulating child labor, and Congress tried once more with the Fair Labor Standards Act of 1938. Among other provisions this law set a sixteen-year minimum age except for hazardous occupations which require eighteen years. Children fourteen and fifteen could work in numerous jobs after school. When this law was tested in the Supreme Court in 1941, the justices reversed

31

their previous ruling and in *U.S. v. Derby Lumber Co.* declared the act legal.

The enlightened attitude toward abolishing child labor was reflected in the 1950 Mid-century White House Conference on Children and Youth. The delegates adopted this recommendation:

"That states and other appropriate public bodies establish and enforce standards covering the employment of youth in all occupations, such standards to include minimum age and wages, as well as hours of work, night work, protection from hazardous occupations, and provisions for workmen's compensation . . ."

All of the states, the District of Columbia, and Puerto Rico now have child labor laws which regulate the employment of children. If both federal and state laws apply, the law setting the higher standards must be observed.

Lest any reader think that child labor is a thing of the past, consider just these three cases cited as recently as 1971:

In Maine a log-driving company employed thirty-three underage boys, some as young as fourteen, to roll logs down the Dead and Kennebec rivers. The boys had been told to falsify their ages so they could be hired for this extremely hazardous work.

On a southern tobacco farm twenty-eight children aged seven to fifteen were found working beneath steaming cheesecloth canopies. They had been hired because the farmer found the space too cramped for mules or adults.

In Detroit a motel-restaurant employed seventy-two minors under sixteen as maids, laundry workers, dishwashers, and in other positions, these children constituting approximately half the work force.

Hamburger stands throughout the country are known

to employ underage workers. One chain was found to have 340 minors working, another 171. The AFL-CIO claimed that there might be as many as "75,000 children, some of them as young as age seven, or eight, or nine, working during school hours or in hazardous occupations."

Catching the violators is not easy, however. The U.S. Department of Labor has only one thousand wage and hour inspectors for the entire nation and is able to investigate "only about 3 percent of the firms" covered by the law.

CHINESE EXCLUSION

Many Chinese laborers started coming to the United States following the discovery of gold in 1848. Between 1864 and 1869 thousands of coolies immigrated to help build the Central Pacific Railroad which pushed east from California. In 1868 the United States and China signed the Burlingame Treaty which protected the right of Chinese to enter the United States.

Soon many Americans were accusing the Chinese of unfair business competition because they worked for lower wages. During the depression of the 1870's there was widespread agitation that immigration be stopped. In spite of the Burlingame Treaty, Congress adopted the first Oriental Exclusion Act of 1882 which barred Chinese laborers from this country. Although the act was supposed to be temporary it was made permanent in 1902.

Meanwhile many Japanese also were coming to the west coast during the late 1880's to settle on farms, where they created serious competition for American farmers. In 1907 a "gentleman's agreement" was negotiated with Japan to restrict immigration, but the terms were unsatisfactory to

Civil Service

many Americans living in the west. As a result of their protests, the Immigration Act of 1924 forbade the entry of all Asian laborers.

The laws against the Chinese immigrants were repealed during World War II, and the Immigration and Nationality Act of 1952 did the same for other Asians (including Japanese) so that thereafter they could enter the United States under a quota and become citizens.

CIVIL SERVICE

Civil service is a system for selecting employees for government service and later promoting them on the basis of merit for the work they do, not whom they know. The federal government, most states and some cities have their own civil service commissions which study each job that is to be filled, decide what knowledge, skills, and particular qualities are necessary, and prepare and give tests to all who qualify. Applicants who show the most proficiency are selected for the vacancies. Civil service was established to assure equal opportunity for all who apply for jobs in the federal government, most states, cities, and counties.

CIVILIAN CONSERVATION CORPS

It was estimated that when President Franklin D. Roosevelt took office approximately fifteen million men and women were unemployed. One of the first measures the new president proposed was the Civilian Conservation Corps for unemployed males between the ages of eighteen and twenty-five. The youth were housed in work camps scattered from coast to coast, and each of the "CCC's" (as the men were known) received one dollar a day, most of which was paid to dependent relatives.

About 250,000 men were enrolled at first and two years later the number was doubled. Before the project was abolished in 1942, more than two million had served in the corps. A great deal of useful work was accomplished in flood control programs, reforestation, highway construction, national parks improvement, and soil conservation.

CLAYTON ACT

In 1914 Congress passed the Clayton Act which Samuel Gompers of the AFL hailed as labor's "Magna Carta." This law strengthened previous antitrust laws and added important sections which affected the rights of labor.

"The labor of a human being is not a commodity or article of commerce," the law declared, as it made certain that antitrust laws should not be used to forbid the existence of unions. It also outlawed the use of injunctions in disputes between management and labor "unless necessary to prevent irreparable injury to property or to a property right . . . for which injury there is no adequate remedy at law."

CLEVELAND, GROVER   **1720276**

Grover Cleveland (1837–1908), the twenty-second and twenty-fourth president of the United States, served his second term (1893–1897) during troubled times. Businesses failed, unemployment grew, banks closed, and social turmoil was widespread during the Panic of 1893. Cleveland lost much of his popularity in 1894, first when he dismissed Coxey's Army of unemployed men who marched to Washington, and later when he crushed the Pullman strike.

When wages were reduced at the Pullman Palace Car Company plant near Chicago, the workers walked off their jobs. The strike spread to every midwestern railroad and soon led to riots. Without the approval of Governor John Altgeld of Illinois, President Cleveland sent federal troops to Chicago on July 6, 1894 to deal with the strikers. A week later the strike had been broken, but not before federal troops had fired on workers for the first time in American labor history and the strikers had caused an estimated $80,000,000 loss just in property damages.

The President was severely criticized by supporters of organized labor, states' rights advocates, and many conservatives because he had jailed the strike leaders by resorting to a blanket injunction rather than requesting a trial and conviction by jury.

(See also: Pullman Strike.)

CLOSED SHOP

Only members of a union may be hired in a closed shop, and in some companies the union furnishes all of the employees. Thus, when additional or replacement workers are needed, the employer requests the union headquarters to send applicants for consideration. The Taft-Hartley Act declared the closed shop illegal.

In a union shop employees do not have to belong to a labor union before they are hired, but each new employee must join the union within a stipulated time after commencing work in order to keep his job.

COAL STRIKES

Coal miners have probably had to endure more strikes than any other group of workers. Until comparatively recent times, the average miner could ill afford a strike because his wages were usually so low that he had no savings and his union was unable to provide much help. Miners were continuously exploited by the mine owners and received little or no sympathy from the press. Thus the plight of the miner meant little or nothing to the average American except that when the miner went out on strike, the price of coal might be forced up and a dangerous fuel scarcity created.

The 1874 Strike. In 1874 anthracite miners in eastern Pennsylvania formed a union, the Miners' and Mine Laborers' Benevolent Association, and reached an agreement with the Anthracite Board of Trade, but in December of that year, despite the agreement, mine owners cut wages below the agreed upon minimum. The miners walked out and widespread violence erupted, caused mostly by a group of men known as Molly Maguires who were partly encouraged by the coal operators themselves. It was not until the following fall that police tracked down the troublemakers and restored peace in the coal fields. By this time the destitute miners were compelled to return to work on the companies' terms and the union virtually collapsed.

The 1902 Strike. In 1902 the United Mine Workers (UMW) made several demands on the operators to cover their principal grievances. The pay was low for a ten-hour day, work was sporadic with average earnings totaling less than $300 a year, accidents were frequent, and companies did nothing to promote mine safety or reimburse miners for expenses or time lost due to accidents. Worse than the pay and working conditions was the so-called feudal system which mine operators had instituted in order to keep the men under their control. Samuel Gompers wrote that the miners "were brought into the world by the company doctor, lived in a company house or hut, were nurtured by the company store . . . laid away in the company graveyard."

The operators refused to discuss the grievances and when the men struck brought four thousand police and deputies into the area to protect the strikebreakers. False charges of riots, violence, and destruction of company property were used to incite public opinion against the

Coal Strikes

UMW and to justify the use of state militia. Actually the miners stayed quietly at home and held firm although there soon was suffering in almost every family.

George F. Baer, spokesman for the operators, was determined to break the union and reject the UMW's arbitration offer. As the operators refused to budge or make a single gesture of conciliation, coal stocks sank in spite of the efforts of strikebreakers. Finally President Theodore Roosevelt summoned Baer and John Mitchell, the UMW leader, to the White House on October 3, 1905. Baer rebuked the President for interfering and nothing was accomplished.

The President then decided to seize and run the mines. He sent the Secretary of War to inform J.P. Morgan, the Wall Street financier behind the operators, that this would be done if arbitration were not accepted. The operators bowed to the president and on October 23 the men returned to work. The following March the President's Anthracite Coal Strike Commission announced a 10 percent wage increase, an eight or nine-hour day for different groups of workers, and establishment of a special board to settle disputes. Union recognition was not gained, although the UMW position was greatly strengthened.

The 1919 Strike. In 1919 the UMW asked for a 60 percent wage increase and a thirty-hour week. The operators said "no" and on November 1 some 425,000 miners refused to work. President Woodrow Wilson secured a court injunction which prohibited further strike activity by union officials and instructed them to cancel the strike order. The acting president, John L. Lewis, in ignoring the advice of the AFL not to obey the court, said: "We are Americans, we cannot fight our government."

Although Lewis cancelled the strike the miners remained at home, refusing to return until granted a wage increase. They did not win any reduction in hours, however. The strike was important because it involved the use of an injunction and set an important precedent for the coal fields.

The 1941 Strike. The John L. Lewis who asserted that "we cannot fight our government" later became the nation's most militant union leader. In 1941 he defied the President when he took his miners out on strike over the issue of establishing a union shop in "captive" coal mines owned and operated by the steel industry.

The 1943 Strike. Two years later, in the midst of World War II, the miners walked off their jobs even before their contracts had expired. President Franklin D. Roosevelt seized the mines and appealed to the miners by radio to return to work. "Tomorrow the Stars and Stripes will fly over the coal mines," he said, "I hope every miner will be at work under that flag." Twenty minutes before the president spoke on the radio, Lewis decided on a fifteen-day truce and for the next six months the controversy dragged on, work stoppages alternating with truces.

The 1946 Strike. Again in May of 1946 the miners stayed home. When only a three week supply of coal remained, an embargo was placed on all freight transportation, and cities ordered brown-outs to save fuel for their gas and lighting utilities. The government seized the mines and worked out a settlement with the UMW but by fall the nation faced another crisis. The miners and operators had not been able to negotiate a contract to replace the temporary agreement signed with the government, and the miners struck, muttering their long-standing motto of: "no contract, no work."

This time the government sought an injunction, but

Coal Strikes

Lewis argued that the Norris-LaGuardia Act of 1932 prohibited use of injunctions in labor disputes.* Finally Judge T. Alan Goldsborough ruled that this law did not apply and that a government could do whatever was necessary to save society from "a public calamity." When Lewis refused to obey he, personally, was fined $10,000 and the UMW $3,500,000.

The case was quickly appealed to the Supreme Court, but before the justices could consider the matter, Lewis ordered a truce. The Court upheld Judge Goldsborough in his action but reduced the fine for the union to $700,000, provided the strike was permanently called off. Lewis agreed and the matter was settled the following year.

The 1948, 1949 and 1950 Strikes. Coal miners put down their tools in each of these three years, and in 1950 the government again instituted contempt proceedings against the union. Before the mines were seized, however, Lewis reached agreement with the operators and the strike was cancelled.

Miners have struck on many other occasions and will continue to do so as long as they are unable to resolve their differences with the operators. In recent years the miners' most important grievances have not been pay or hours of work but safety. On November 20, 1968 an explosion in one of the Consolidated Coal Company's mines killed seventy-eight men. This was not an isolated incident. During the next three years 657 other miners lost their lives underground.

"Black lung," an occupational disease which has hit as many as 300,000 miners is another critical issue. On December 31, 1969 President Richard Nixon signed the Fed-

---

* The law also forbade the use of "yellow-dog" contracts.

eral Coal Mine Health and Safety Act. This set mine-safety standards and established a black lung compensation program to provide monthly cash benefits for miners disabled by pneumonoconiosis and for widows of miners who died of the disease.

The law did not solve all the problems, however. Miners complained that violators of the coal-safety rules received token fines for continuing to endanger their workers' lives. Furthermore, half the miners who had the black lung disease were ruled ineligible for benefits because they were not considered totally disabled.

Arnold Miller, a retired miner and president of the Black Lung Association which miners formed to lobby for benefits, summed up the miners' philosophy when he said: "Strikes are the only real weapon miners have."

(See also: John L. Lewis; John Mitchell; United Mine Workers.)

CODE OF ETHICS

One of the problems which faced the AFL-CIO after the two federations merged in 1955 was how to deal with the unethical (if not downright criminal) practices of several affiliated unions. Some labor leaders were accused of borrowing or taking union funds (particularly pension and welfare money) for their own use. Some officials were known to have threatened employers with trouble and thereby extorted money from them. Others had resorted to violence to get what they wanted.

The AFL-CIO established an Ethical Practices Committee to draft and enforce codes of conduct, but some of the unions were so notoriously corrupt that in 1957 Congress voted to set up the Select Committee on Improper Activities in the Labor or Management Field. Under the chairmanship of Senator John L. McClellan of Arkansas, the

McClellan Committee as it came to be known, conducted investigations of many witnesses and uncovered shocking evidence of union corruption and criminalities.

As a result of these revelations the AFL-CIO expelled the Teamsters Union, the Laundry Workers, and the Bakery and Confectionery Workers in 1957. The following March the McClellan Committee published its first report, after which President Dwight Eisenhower asked for legislation to stop "corruption, racketeering, and abuse of trust and power in labor-management relations." Congress passed the Labor-Management Reporting and Disclosure Act of 1959, or the Landrum-Griffin Act as it was more popularly known.

(See also: Dave Beck; Landrum-Griffin Act.)

COLLECTIVE BARGAINING

This is considered one of the most fundamental and important elements in good labor-management relations. The term refers not only to the negotiations which must take place between labor and management before an agreement can be reached on wages, hours of work, and other matters relating to employment, but it also covers the administration and interpretation of the contract once it has been signed.

Collective bargaining is conducted by representatives of a company and a union who meet to discuss various issues such as wages, hours, fringe benefits, seniority, handling of grievances, and other problems. The usual procedure is for the union to announce its demands, after which management studies them and makes a counter offer. The two sides then meet until they are able to work out an agreement, each side generally having to increase, modify, or give up some of its requests or proffers. Negotiations may last many days or even weeks; once agreement has been reached, the terms are set forth and published in the form of a written contract. A typical document sets forth all of the provisions which have been agreed upon affecting wages, hours, and other conditions of employment. An important element in most contracts deals with union security, the company's promise to require that all employees covered by the contract must belong to the union.

Company-wide collective bargaining covers all of a company's employees; *plant-wide* collective bargaining includes employees in one plant although the company may operate numerous other plants; *industry-wide* (or *multi-employer*) collective bargaining covers a majority of the union members in an industry; *area-wide* collective bargaining covers negotiations conducted between representatives of management and labor for two or more industries.

COMMITTEE OF FIFTY

In 1829 some employers in New York City threatened to restore the eleven-hour day although this was the only city in which trade unionists had won a ten-hour working day. Under the leadership of Thomas Skidmore, a mechanic, union leaders met on April 23 to discuss how they could combat the threat and then called a mass meeting a few days later. Some five thousand workingmen turned out and declared that they would not work more than the "just and reasonable time of ten hours a day." A strike fund of a hundred dollars was raised and a Committee of Fifty was appointed to conduct the fight.

The employers were so frightened by this action that they dropped their threat, but the Committee of Fifty continued to meet, concentrating their attention on other labor problems and politics. That October another mass meeting was called to present a labor platform to the

43

workingmen; they showed no enthusiasm for Skidmore's ideas, although they voted to take political action which called for the formation of a party and preparation of a workingman's ticket in the coming November elections.

The new organization, the New York Workingmen's Party, put up a slate of nominees, all but two of whom were journeymen. A carpenter, Ebenezer Ford, was elected to the state assembly and every candidate received a minimum of 6,000 of the 21,000 votes cast. Shortly thereafter Skidmore, who was not popular with the workingmen, formed the Equal Rights Party, and the Committee of Fifty and the Workingmen's Party disappeared by 1832.

(See also: Equal Rights Movement; Workingmen's Parties.)

COMMUNISTS IN THE LABOR MOVEMENT

Communists have always tried to infiltrate labor unions in order to have direct contacts with the workingman. Prior to the 1930's the Red sympathizers had little influence in the United States. The most radical union was the Industrial Workers of the World (IWW) but it disintegrated during the early 1920's. By 1930 some Communists had risen to important positions in several unions, especially in the needle trades.

As the depression of the 1930's worsened the Communists became more active. They sympathized with and provided some aid to the unemployed but devoted most of their efforts to encouraging workers to revolt against the capitalist system. Most Americans ignored them, but when the CIO planned its first campaign to recruit members, many Communists were hired to help organize the non-union industries. The Communists were known for their willingness to work hard; nothing stopped them from gaining their objectives and soon they occupied key posts in several large unions.

During World War II the United States and Russia both fought Germany and during that time the Communists in this country caused no trouble. With the start of the Cold War * in the late 1940's, however, most of the Communists in top union positions turned their loyalties to the Communist Party rather than to their unions. Public hostility grew and there was also widespread agitation in the ranks of labor to oust them from their posts.

In 1947 Walter Reuther expelled the Communist leaders of the United Automobile Workers and Joseph Curran of the Maritime Union removed those associates who were known to be Reds. In 1949 the CIO revised its constitution to bar Communists from executive offices and to banish any union which was Communist dominated. The United Electrical, Radio and Machine Workers was immediately ejected, followed the next year by ten more affiliates. New unions were quickly organized to take the place of those expelled.

Company Union

A company union is an organization of workers which is sponsored by the employer. The usual purpose is to keep outside unions from organizing the employees as well as to assure a dependable and willing labor supply.

The Nernst Lamp Co. of Pittsburgh is thought to have started the first company union in 1901. Two years later the Brotherhood of Motormen and the Brotherhood of Conductors were organized by the Everett Syndicate

---

* The name given to the poor American-Soviet relations which developed after 1946. Although there was no outright war, a number of hostile diplomatic battles often seemed about to bring the two countries to the brink of actual warfare.

which operated a network of street railway routes in Ohio. A company Trades and Workers' Association was forced on employees of the Post Cereal Company in 1907 by C. W. Post who strongly advocated the open shop.

After the coal miners' strike of 1914, the movement to form company unions gained momentum. In most cases, when employees joined these organizations they had to declare that they would not strike or join in any labor dispute and that they opposed the AFL and other trade unions. They also had to acknowledge the need for strong cooperation between capital and labor. Company unions were doomed in 1933 when the National Labor Relations Act guaranteed employees the right to organize and bargain collectively.

COMPULSORY LABOR

The principle of compulsory labor was adopted by all of the American colonies. Idleness was punished by whipping and fines. Those who would not work were sent to the workhouse, while newcomers who could not find employment were sent back to the colony from which they came. The various towns required all able men between sixteen and sixty to work on the roads a certain number of days each year, and during wartime those males not serving in the militia might be forced to labor on farms.

During the middle of the eighteenth century, many colonial towns established manufacturing enterprises to provide jobs for the unemployed and for those children whose parents could not support them. Compulsory labor was the rule for all males whether they were self-employed, wage earners, or laborers in the workhouses or public manufacturing plants.

46

CONCILIATION

The dictionary definition of this term refers to the act of bringing people together, soothing their anger, and placating them. In the area of labor relations, some experts define the word as meaning the negotiating machinery which exists for settling disputes between management and labor wherein outsiders do not participate. Other experts think of conciliation as the act of a conciliator from the outside who brings parties together and presides over their meetings but makes no recommendations. Since conciliation has no binding force on the disputing parties, it may have little value, especially if they cannot come to an agreement.

The Federal Mediation and Conciliation Service was created by the Labor Management Relations Act of 1947. The Service possesses no law enforcement authority, and its mediators rely wholly on persuasive techniques of mediation and conciliation to perform their duties. Their purpose is to assist disputant parties in industries affecting interstate commerce to settle such disputes through conciliation and mediation.

(See also: Arbitration; Mediation.)

CONGRESS OF INDUSTRIAL ORGANIZATIONS

For years there was dissension within the AFL because many members felt strongly that mass production workers should be included the same as unions of craftsmen. After unions received the undisputed legal right in 1933 to organize workers, John L. Lewis, head of the miners' union, led a group within the AFL which declared that workers in mass production industries should have mass industrial unions. In 1935 eight union leaders formed the Committee for Industrial Organization within the AFL to achieve this goal.

Congress of Industrial Organizations

The next year Philip Murray set up a Steel Workers Organizing Committee which signed up thousands of steel workers and by year end had established 150 locals with 100,000 members. In 1937 John L. Lewis had negotiated a contract with the United States Steel Corporation (which had led the antiunion movement for the past four decades) and by December of that year the CIO had the following membership: 100,000 agricultural and packinghouse workers, 400,000 automobile workers, 175,000 clothing workers, 250,000 ladies' garment workers, 600,000 miners, 80,000 rubber workers and 375,000 steel workers, or a total of 3,700,000 members.

This activity precipitated a split within the ranks of the AFL as old-time leaders opposed this new organization and insisted on maintaining the craft-type structure. In May, 1938, all the unions which had associated with the new committee were expelled from the AFL. In order to maintain continuity, the new federation kept the same initials, CIO, but changed its name to Congress of Industrial Organizations.

The CIO became far more vocal and sponsored more extensive political activities than the conservative AFL. It also included other types of unions besides the industrial ones. Some of its affiliates were accused of being Communist dominated which hurt the CIO's reputation. In 1950 seven such affiliates were expelled.

As early as 1946 leaders of the AFL and CIO began to discuss the desirability and possibility of a merger. From time to time talks were continued and in 1951 the two organizations formed the United Labor Policy Committee to coordinate labor's participation in the Korean War effort. The following year George Meany and Walter Reuther, the new presidents of the AFL and CIO respectively, both publicly stated their desire to effect a union.

By this time many of the AFL leaders who had opposed merger were gone, and more than half of the AFL members were now in industrial unions. More important, the Republican victory of 1952 warned of a possible antilabor drive and this gave new impetus to a merger. Leaders of both federations decided that they had more to gain by merging than by continuing their rivalry, and in December of 1955 the 10,500,000 AFL and 4,500,000 CIO members joined to form the AFL-CIO. Leadership was vested in George Meany as president with Walter Reuther as second in command.

(See also: American Federation of Labor.)

CONSUMER PRICE INDEX

The Bureau of Labor Statistics of the U.S. Department of Labor compiles this index monthly. It represents a statistical measurement of the price changes in some four hundred commodities and services such as clothing, entertainment, food, medical care, rent, transportation, and other family expenditures which are purchased by clerical workers and wage earners who live in fifty-six areas. All of the prices are combined to make an index number.

The index shows only percentage changes in prices. Each of these changes is expressed as a percentage of the base period, which is an average of the years 1957-1959. In an index of this kind, the base period is said to equal 100 and any increases or decreases in prices will be compared to that base period as a percent of 100. Thus, if the price index stands at 110, it means that consumer prices have risen 10 percent above the 1957-1959 base.

The wholesale price index shows changes in prices of approximately 2,400 commodities such as chemicals, farm products, fuels, leather, lumber, machinery, metals, paper, rubber, and textile products which are bought by wholesale businesses. It measures prices against a base of 1957–1959 in the same way as the Consumer Price Index.

Sometimes union contracts contain clauses which provide that future wage increases will be based on the consumer price index.

(See also: Cost of Living.)

CONTRACT LABOR ACT

Congress passed the Contract Labor Act of 1864 to obtain additional labor needed during the Civil War. The law provided that Europeans might be brought into the United States if they promised to sign over not more than twelve months wages to repay the cost of bringing them here. The American Emigrant Company was then formed to import workingmen for ". . . manufacturers, railroad companies and other employers."

The aliens were unskilled and inefficient but useful to manufacturers who lacked workers to operate machines and to companies which sought muscle power. The National Labor Union blamed these aliens for much of the unemployment which followed the Civil War and accused employers of using them as strikebreakers. In 1868 Congress repealed the act.

COST OF LIVING

This term refers to the prices people must pay for the goods and services they buy. Since World War II, the cost of living in the United States has been rising, with the result that the value of the dollar has been decreasing steadily.

The Bureau of Labor Statistics measures the cost of living by preparing two monthly price indexes: The

Consumer Price Index and the Wholesale Price Index. (See also: Consumer Price Index.)

CRAFT UNION

This term refers to a labor union which represents only workers who perform the same type of work such as carpenters, painters, bakers, etc. (It is also called a horizontal union.) The AFL originally limited its affiliates to craft unions.

(See also: American Federation of Labor.)

CRAFTSMEN

An artisan, mechanic, or one who is engaged in a particular craft is known as a craftsman. Prior to the industrial revolution craftsmen produced most of the commodities required for everyday living. With the growth of colonial towns along the Atlantic seaboard, the demand for craftsmen increased. Hatters, shoemakers, tailors, cabinet-makers, weavers, masons, carpenters, bakers, and printers were among those who had their own businesses or shops and employed journeymen and apprentices.

(See also: Apprenticeship.)

CRISPINS

This was a national craft union of shoemakers known as the Knights of St. Crispin (there were also the Daughters of St. Crispin). The Knights were named for two brothers, Crispin and Crispinian, who were early Christian martyrs and became the patron saints of shoemakers because they had followed that trade. The union was organized in 1867 when labor saving machinery was introduced and threatened employment in the shoe industry.

The new union grew rapidly and numbered fifty thousand members by 1870 but declined just as rapidly as the union lost one strike after another. Inexperienced workers called "green hands" were employed to operate the new machines and the Knights refused to work next to them. By the time the depression of 1873 set in the union had become defunct.

CURRAN, JOSEPH EDWIN

This maritime labor leader was born on New York City's East Side on March 1, 1906. He went to sea when he was sixteen but during the 1930 Depression lost his job and was forced to wash dishes to earn his living, often sleeping in the park or at the Seaman's Institute. In 1935 he joined the AFL's International Seaman's Union (ISU) which was then in a turmoil because many members were protesting the $5 higher monthly pay given west coast sailors who made $62.50 a month.

The following year Curran sailed to San Pedro on the *California*, owned by the International Mercantile Marine Company (IMMC). He soon assumed leadership of the crew and upon arrival in port, told the IMMC that the men would not return to New York unless they received west coast rates. Both the president of the company and the Secretary of Commerce, Dan Roper, called it mutiny and the ISU censured the action. The matter was settled when Frances Perkins, Secretary of Labor, left a White House dinner to call Curran in San Pedro. She promised she would try to get the extra $5 without discrimination against further employment of Curran or the other men.

When the *California* returned to New York, the IMMC immediately fired and blacklisted the twenty-five crew members. Thereupon Curran and the other men picketed the *California* and other intercoastal vessels and announced several strike aims. The ISU expelled Curran, calling him a Communist. After two months the strike was cancelled because it was ineffective. Later that year Curran organized a Seaman's Defense Committee and called a strike which crippled the entire American maritime industry.

The next year, 1937, Curran formed the National Maritime Union (NMU) and won representation on fifty-two shipping lines. He was then elected president of the NMU, and with many Communists in top positions, the union affiliated with the CIO. Following World War II Curran ousted those union leaders who were known to be Communists. Meanwhile he had been elected a vice-president of the CIO in 1941 and assumed the same post with the AFL-CIO in 1955.

D

DEBS, EUGENE VICTOR

This labor leader and founder of the Socialist Party was born in Terre Haute, Indiana, November 5, 1855. At the age of fifteen he became a locomotive fireman after working in the Terre Haute railroad shop. He assisted in organizing the local lodge of the Brotherhood of Locomotive Firemen and became associate editor of the Brotherhood's *Firemen's Magazine.* In 1880 when elected national secretary and treasurer he also became editor of the magazine. Debs served as city clerk of Terre Haute from 1879–1883, and the following year was elected to the Indiana legislature where he sat from 1885–1892.

Debs opposed the AFL with its groupings by crafts, believing that it was preferable to organize labor by industry. In 1893 he founded and became first president of the American Railway Union (ARU) and within a year his board had declared a sympathetic strike to help the Pullman Company workers in Chicago. Held in contempt of court for violating a federal injunction, the labor leader received a six month sentence. During this time he read widely on socialism, was visited by Victor L. Berger, and left prison a convert to socialism.

In 1897 he led what was left of the ARU into the Social Democratic Party of America which later became the Socialist Party of America. Debs ran for president as a Socialist in 1900, 1904, 1908, 1912, and 1920, polling more than 900,000 votes or nearly 6 percent of the ballots cast in 1912. Meanwhile he helped form the Industrial Workers of the World but withdrew subsequently because he was not sympathetic with the radical views of the other leaders.

Debs' opposition to America's entry into World War I resulted in his receiving a ten year jail sentence for sedition. Although Debs was still in prison at the time of the presidential election of 1920, he received almost a million votes. The following Christmas Day President Warren Harding pardoned the socialist leader, and thereafter Debs worked to improve prison conditions. He published *Walls and Bars,* a book which dealt with prison conditions and problems.

Debs was convinced that socialism was the best cure for all that was wrong with capitalism which he considered a great evil. His untiring devotion to the Socialist Party, his sincerity, integrity, and friendliness won him countless friends and followers, although most workers did not agree with his socialist ideas. He died in Elmhurst, Illinois on October 20, 1926.

DE LEON, DANIEL

This journalist and socialist leader was born in Curaçao, Netherlands Antilles, on December 14, 1852. He studied in Germany and Holland, then emigrated to New York City in 1872. Here he taught school and edited a Cuban revolutionist periodical and obtained his law degree at Columbia University in 1878. He lectured at Columbia in Latin American diplomacy, joined the Socialist Labor Party in 1890, and as editor of the party's publication, *The People,* dominated the party and expounded his belief in the Marxist principles. At the same time he opposed trade union leaders and advocated establishment of socialist unions based on industries, not crafts like the AFL. In 1890 and 1902 he ran unsuccessfully as the Socialist Labor candidate for Governor of New York.

In 1895 De Leon established the Socialist Trade and Labor Alliance, but four years later most of the members resigned to join with Eugene V. Debs who was forming the new Socialist Party. The so-called De Leonites now lost any influence they might have had, and in 1905 De Leon joined with Debs and William Haywood to organize the Industrial Workers of the World (IWW) and merged the remnant of his group with them. Three years later, a faction of the IWW seized power and expelled De Leon and others who advocated political rather than revolutionary action. To retaliate, De Leon formed the Workers' International Industrial Union which proved ineffective and served only as a mouthpiece for his ideas.

Although De Leon's real influence on the labor movement was minimal, he was a well-known figure in the socialist movement. He published two books on socialist theory: *Two Pages from Roman History* (1903) and *Socialist Reconstruction of Society* (1905). He died on May 11, 1914.

(See also: Industrial Workers of the World, Socialist Party of America.)

DEPRESSION OF THE 1930'S

The Great Depression of the 1930's followed a period when there was excessive bank lending plus wild speculation in stocks, land and building. Because the stock market steadily surged upward and investors were making profits, many Americans did not realize what was really happening. Iron and steel production, automobile output and building construction were slowing down. At the same time activity in the mining, agriculture and lumbering industries had slackened and general unemployment had increased. Finally, prices on the stock market tumbled in the fall of 1929 and ruined many people. The general business depression which followed then spread to other countries.

Countless Americans suffered privation and hunger during the Great Depression. At one time it was estimated that some fifteen million were out of work. The federal government introduced massive public works projects to provide jobs for the unemployed and orders for idle factories. The end came when World War II began in 1939. This stimulated widespread defense production as private industry hired workers formerly employed on government projects. The economy quickly recovered and a long-time business boom gradually returned the country to prosperity.

DISCRIMINATION IN HIRING

Discrimination in hiring has always been a problem for Negroes and other minority races. Discrimination can spell tragedy to the man whose color or race bars him from a job. In many places discrimination in hiring still exists in spite of all the sincere efforts that have been made to abolish it.

Many states have enacted antidiscrimination laws, forbidding any reference to color or race when hiring, but they have proven difficult to enforce. In 1962 one hundred of the nation's largest unions signed agreements with the President's Committee on Equal Employment Opportunity to end discrimination within their ranks. Unions stated that signing the agreements was proof of their intent to honor their long-standing promise to improve Negro job opportunities.

Anxious to see results instead of continued promises, Roy Wilkins, Executive Secretary of the National Association for the Advancement of Colored People (NAACP), filed charges of discrimination with the National Labor Relations Board in 1962. The AFL-CIO asserted that these accusations were "baseless" and liable to strain relations between the NAACP and the AFL-CIO. President George Meany of the AFL-CIO contended that there undoubtedly was discrimination at the local level of unions but that machinery was available to cope with the problem and that it would be better to settle matters that way rather than to file complaints with the government.

Since that time economic boycotts against stores or companies that did not hire Negroes or denied Negroes advancement and job equality have been fairly effective. Sit-ins and public demonstrations which often led to violence have also been employed with varying degrees of success.

57

Discrimination in Hiring

The real answer appeared to lie in effective legislation which was the original intent of the Congress when it considered the Civil Rights Act of 1964. This law aimed to eliminate all employment discrimination based on color, race, sex, and religion in industries engaged in interstate commerce. After its fourth year the law covered all employers of at least twenty-five workers.

The act established the Equal Employment Opportunity Commission (EEOC) which was to administer and enforce the fair employment practice sections of the statute. To mollify southern objection, the EEOC was not given any power to enforce the act. It could investigate complaints of job discrimination but the best it could do was to try to bring about a voluntary settlement of a dispute. If that failed, the individual who sought justice had to file suit in court. Actually this meant that most workers who had suffered discrimination were financially unable to undertake costly court proceedings and therefore had no hope of winning any help. The EEOC could recommend that the U.S. Attorney General file suits against violators but this did not prove practical.

Civil rights groups and women's organizations pressed Congress to give the EEOC authority to enforce the law, but it was not until 1972 that a new act was adopted to do this. Again objection of southern Senators made it necessary to work out a compromise, but this time the EEOC was authorized to take cases to federal court to obtain an order that would stop discriminatory hiring and promotion policies. The Commission's authority was broadened to cover government workers and employees of educational institutions as well as companies with as few as 15 employees and unions representing 15 or more members.

Here at last was help not only for minority groups but

58

also for women who over the years had been discriminated against in job hiring, in receiving equal pay for equal work, and in receiving promotion into supervisory positions as readily as men.

DISTRICT 50

The United Mine Workers of America is organized into 28 districts, all involving the coal industry except District 50, which was made a general catch-all union.

Once labor unions were free to organize workers in the mid-1930's, John L. Lewis, president of the United Mine Workers, initiated an aggressive campaign not only to build up the union's membership in the coal fields, but in other industries also. Initially District 50 was interested in organizing the chemical industry, but the recruiters ranged far and wide, at one time even signing up dairy farmers on the basis of 10¢ a cow.

District 50 is an international union with a wide membership in highway construction, manufacturing, service, and other industries.

(See also: John L. Lewis; United Mine Workers of America.)

DRAFT RIOTS

In mid-July 1863, the nation experienced several destructive and bloody draft riots as mobs rampaged through New York City for three days, killing a number of Negroes and destroying railroads, shipyards, factories, machine shops and homes. Elsewhere, in Troy, New York, and towns in Indiana, Pennsylvania, and Wisconsin, workingmen were active in rioting and showing their anger at the Conscription Act of 1863.

This legislation made it possible for a person to evade military service by providing a substitute or paying three hundred dollars. Workingmen felt that this discriminated against them; they also fell prey to Copperhead * propaganda that the purpose of the war was "to enable abolitionist Capitalists to transport Negroes into the northern cities to replace . . . workers who were striking for higher wages."

In spite of its fears and hatred for the Conscription Act, labor remained loyal during the war and supported the government.

DUBINSKY, DAVID

This famous labor leader was born in Brest Litovsk, Poland, on February 22, 1892. His father moved the family to Lodz where he rented rooms in a basement and at night turned the kitchen into a bakery. David, the youngest of six children, started working for his father at thirteen. Two years later he joined the bakers' union, whereupon he was elected secretary because he could read and write. When the bakers struck for higher wages, David led pickets in front of his father's shop. He was also active as a revolutionary Socialist, conspiring against the Czarist government in Poland. At sixteen he was arrested because of his political activities and sentenced to a Siberian prison.

Escaping from prison, he made his way back to Lodz and hid from the police until his brother Jacob could give him a steamship ticket for New York. His first job was as a dishwasher earning three dollars a week. Evenings he busied himself in Socialist party meetings. He soon became a cloak cutter and joined the International Ladies' Garment Workers' Union Local 10. He rose from general manager and secretary-treasurer of his local in 1921, to secretary of the national union in 1929 and president in 1932, a post he held until 1966.

* Any Northerner who sympathized with the southern states.

The year after Dubinsky's election to the presidency, collective bargaining became legal under the National Industrial Recovery Act and he signed up 160,000 new members within six months. At the same time he reduced the union's debt and by 1935 had built up assets of $850,000 in place of a million dollar debt. That same year he joined John L. Lewis to form the Committee for Industrial Organization, but he opposed establishing the CIO permanently and for a time the ILGWU was not affiliated with either the AFL or CIO.

Meanwhile Dubinsky had left the Socialist Party in 1928 and with Sidney Hillman organized the American Labor Party in 1936. When Communists seized control of the party in 1944, he resigned and with Adolf A. Berle, Jr. and others formed the Liberty Party in New York State. In 1947 he was one of the founders of the Americans for Democratic Action and served on the board.

Dubinsky was one of the shrewdest trade union leaders and in many ways one of the most progressive. His union was once said to have the most complete welfare program in the country. It worked closely with employers to help them run their businesses more efficiently; it settled grievances and had no major strikes for fifteen years. Perhaps a subordinate gave the best description of the tireless president when he said: "Dubinsky is our best editor, best publicity man, best architect, best ticket taker, best seat arranger, best auditor, best economist and best dramatic editor." This unique labor leader who was known for his stand against racketeering, his work in collective bargaining, and his devotion to labor's international affairs, resigned from the union at the age of seventy-four because: "I don't want to die in my boots. I want to be free."

(See also: International Ladies' Garment Workers' Union.)

E

EIGHT-HOUR DAY

Before the Industrial Revolution everyone who worked on farms was expected to labor from sunrise to sunset. The owners imposed the same hours when the first factories started production although the working conditions were often more demanding and difficult.

In the United States the "sunrise to sunset" system was still acceptable to most of the trades in the 1820's. However, many workers were beginning to complain that the hours were unbearable and demanded a working day from six to six with two hours off for eating. This was called the ten-hour day. In 1825 Boston carpenters struck for these hours but the strike failed. In New York City some of the trade associations pushed for a ten-hour day, and because labor was so scarce, employers granted their request. By 1828 New York was known as a "ten-hour town" for skilled labor.

This success was achieved in only a few places until after 1835 when workers from all the trades in Philadelphia went on strike and marched through the streets. After this demonstration the movement spread to other parts of the nation, but in the new factories rising in New England and elsewhere, the twelve-hour day was destined to remain for many years.

In 1844 an investigation ordered by the Massachusetts General Court showed that in textile factories the average working day, depending on the season, varied from eleven hours and twenty-four minutes to thirteen hours and thirty-one minutes. The investigating committee admitted that shorter hours would bring great benefits to the workers but decided that no action should be taken lest industry be driven from the state.

Three years later New Hampshire passed the first ten-hour law and Pennsylvania did the same the following year for workers "in cotton, woolen, silk, paper, bagging and flax factories." Other states soon adopted similar statutes but all of these acts had one feature in common. The ten-hour rule could be avoided by "special contracts." Thus the law might be circumvented by any employer who could refuse to hire a man unless he agreed to sign a special contract to work a longer day. If the employee stood up for his legal rights and refused, he would be blacklisted by all employers.

Following the Civil War, Ira Steward, a Boston machinist and union member, undertook a one-man campaign to push for the eight-hour day. He made innumerable speeches, wrote pamphlets, testified before the Massachusetts legislature, and organized first the Labor Reform Association and then the Grand Eight-Hour League of Massachusetts. Eight-hour leagues sprang up throughout the country and the National Labor Union adopted the program.

As a result of this agitation, the federal government adopted the eight-hour day for mechanics and laborers on public works but never enforced the act. Eight state legislatures also made a gesture toward their employees but included the same loopholes in their new eight-hour laws as they had previously used. Therefore these statutes were meaningless for state employees who still had to work whatever hours their employers stipulated.

Labor unions grew stronger during the 1880's and the eight-hour day became an important issue. In 1886 a movement spread across the United States for general strikes to be held on May 1 to demonstrate in favor of an eight-hour day. The strikes went off peacefully but achieved little, and in Chicago the strike proved the indirect cause of the Haymarket Square Riot a few days later. In October of the same year, some twenty-five thousand packing house workers in the Chicago Union Stock Yards struck when their bosses failed to honor an agreement to give them an eight-hour day with no reduction in pay. Their leader, Terence V. Powderly betrayed them and the strike failed.

Two years later the AFL convention voted to demand an eight-hour day starting May 1, 1890. Mass meetings were to be held on four holidays prior to the deadline and a general strike would be called for May 1, 1890 to enforce the union's demand. The AFL changed its mind, however, and instead of a general strike backed the carpenters' union in their eight-hour drive which they won in 137 cities.

The National Association of Manufacturers was active in opposing all legislation that would have provided for a shorter work week and from 1902–1912 helped secure the defeat of eight federal bills. During this period there were still some industries in which men were forced to work sixteen to eighteen hours a day. This was especially true of street railway employees.

In 1912 Congress passed another federal eight-hour act which covered "workmen employed by contractors and sub-contractors on work done for or on behalf of the Federal Government." Now the eight-hour movement swept across the country and legislation was adopted in many states.

In the case of the four big railroad brotherhoods, the

ten-hour day had been won through strike threats in 1910. When union leaders wanted to obtain the eight-hour day for their members in 1916, they again threatened strike action. President Woodrow Wilson thereupon went before a joint session of Congress to ask for an eight-hour day for trainmen. The Adamson Act of 1916 established eight hours as a standard for all employees working on interstate railroads.

By 1920 most basic industries had accepted the eight-hour day, but it was not until 1923 that the United States Steel Corporation adopted the shorter working hours for its employees.

EMERGENCY RAILROAD TRANSPORTATION ACT

The Emergency Railroad Transportation Act of 1933 recognized the various railway unions as proper bargaining agents and guaranteed all railroad employees the right to organize and bargain collectively.

The law also established the office of Federal Coordinator of Transportation. The Coordinator was directed to conduct various studies and report to the President on elimination of duplication and waste, reorganization of railroad financing, labor relations, means of improving transportation, and other matters. Joseph B. Eastman, a member of the Interstate Commerce Commission, served as coordinator from 1933 until 1936 when the office closed.

EMPLOYERS ASSOCIATIONS

These are associations organized by employers who desire to unite in order to deal with their organized employees. An employers association may be concerned with a single trade or industry, it may be a city or regional federation of many employers associations, or it may be a national organization representing one or more industries. Until unions won the right to organize and bargain collectively with their employers, most of the employers associations had one principal purpose: to prevent the growth of unionism and keep unions out of members' shops. Today these associations work to solve problems which are created by unions and collective bargaining. (See also: Antiunion Campaigns.)

EMPLOYMENT AGENCIES

An employment agency is an organization whose purpose is to bring together employers who have positions to be filled and men and women who are seeking work. Private (or commercial) agencies provide this service for fees which are paid by the employer or the employee. Some of them also offer counseling services. Union hiring halls find jobs for union members in some industries, but the Taft-Hartley Act prohibits discrimination against non-union employees. These agencies have been forced to change their methods of operation to conform to the law.

The most extensive system of employment agencies is operated by the states in cooperation with the federal government. The Wagner-Peyser Act of 1933 created the United States Employment Service which provides leadership to the state employment service agencies. It assists them in establishing and maintaining a system of public employment offices in the states and territories. Through this nation-wide network it is possible for each state employment office to know about all the job openings which are listed with every other office. No fees are charged for using this service.

EQUAL RIGHTS MOVEMENT

During the early 1830's as workingmen were organizing into unions, one of the matters of greatest concern to them was the apparent attempts of the courts and the wealthy elite to degrade the workers into "mere tools to build up princely fortunes for men who grasp at all and produce nothing." Once again the old slogan of "taxation without representation" became popular. The working-men felt that they had no say in how taxes were spent as long as the state legislatures and courts were filled with men unsympathetic to their problems and deaf to their wishes. The equal rights supposedly guaranteed by the Constitution hardly existed for the common man. It was this worry which sparked the so-called equal rights movement.

On September 15, 1836, a convention of ninety-three farmers, mechanics, and workingmen met in Utica, New York. They issued a Declaration of Independence, declaring the independence of workers and farmers from the old political parties. The delegates then voted to form their own political party, the Equal Rights Party, and nominated a slate for governor and lieutenant governor. Soon Equal Rights tickets had been nominated in some twenty counties and a half-dozen newspapers in New York State were supporting the movement. In the fall election this workingmen's party held the balance of power between the Democrats and Whigs and helped elect three of the four candidates for Congress. A state senator and two assemblymen also owed their election to the party. Most important, the Equal Rights Party prevented the New York City Tammany Hall machine from electing their candidates without the support of the workingmen.

This short-lived movement spread to other states where workingmen helped candidates of their choice. Locofoco-

67

ism *, or the Equal Rights movement, had its greatest success in New York State because several of the city trade union constitutions forbade members from engaging in "party politics" and this gave them the opportunity to do so.

(See also: Committee of Fifty; Workingmen's Parties.)

ERDMAN ACT

As a result of the 1894 Pullman Strike, Congress enacted the Erdman Act of 1898 to set up mediation machinery for railroad disputes. Under the law the chairman of the Interstate Commerce Commission and the Commissioner of Labor were named a permanent mediation board whose services were available to railroad labor or management in any dispute. If a settlement could not be reached, the mediators would have to set up a special three man board to propose arbitration and, if this procedure were accepted, the board's decision would be binding on both parties.

The law also outlawed the use of all yellow-dog contracts by the railroads. In these contracts employees agreed not to join a union during the period they were employed. The Supreme Court declared this provision unconstitutional in 1908 in the case of *Adair v. United States*. The court held that the law was unwarranted interference with the freedom to make a contract as well as an invasion of liberty and rights of property. Again in 1915

* Locofoco was the name applied to the radical or Equal Rights section of the Democratic Party. It originated at a meeting held in Tammany Hall on October 29, 1835 when there was a dispute. The chairman left his seat, the gas lights were extinguished to dissolve the meeting, but those in favor of extreme measures used locofoco matches, a recent invention, to light candles they had brought with them. They then continued the meeting and attained their objectives. Newspapers later called this faction the Locofoco Party.

in the case of *Coppage v. Kansas,* the Supreme Court struck down a comparable state statute.

EVANS, GEORGE HENRY

This journalist and land reformer was born in Bromyard, England, on March 25, 1805. He emigrated to the United States in 1820 where he and his brother Frederick came under the influence of Thomas Paine and before long were "militant freethinkers and reformers." In 1829 the Evans brothers published the first important labor paper in this country, *The Working Man's Advocate.* They reported activities of Workingmen's Parties then being formed in Philadelphia, New York, and other cities, and urged support of Workingmen's tickets. George Evans edited this paper for workers at various times from 1828–1845, stating that the publication was "designed solely to protect and advance their interests."

Frederick Evans left the publishing business to become a Shaker elder, while George, now an atheist, continued writing, publishing pamphlets and also editing the *Daily Sentinel* and *Young America* occasionally between 1837 and 1853. For a time he withdrew from his journalism work and then resumed editing and writing in 1841 when he pushed aggressively for a land distribution program which maintained that every person should be given a homestead of 160 acres in order to relieve urban congestion. He also spoke out against slavery, imprisonment for debt, monopoly and discrimination against women, and demanded numerous reforms to aid the labor movement.

In 1844 Evans campaigned for free homesteads, and it was said that the Homestead Act of 1862 was adopted partly because of the work he had done to educate the public to this idea. He died in Granville, N.J. on February 2, 1856.

F ••

FACTORY SYSTEM

The factory system appeared during the eighteenth century with the advent of the industrial revolution when the manufacturing process was introduced and workers no longer labored at home but in factories. Instead of working for themselves, artisans now were hired for wages to operate machines, transferring their skills from making handcrafts to machine made products.

The new system required capital to purchase buildings and machinery, plentiful labor to staff the plants, mechanical power such as steam or water to replace man power, and machines to take the place of human skills in order to turn out goods. Although the system increased production, it created serious economic and social problems for the workers. It not only caused a concentration of industry, housing congestion, smoke pollution, and sanitation problems, but also was indirectly responsible for the increase of juvenile delinquency and the early breakdown of the family.

(See also: Industrial Revolution.)

FAIR LABOR STANDARDS ACT

This law, also known as the Wages and Hours Law, was adopted by Congress on June 25, 1938, and covered all workers in businesses engaged in interstate commerce or producing goods for interstate commerce. A milestone in labor relations legislation, its purpose was to eliminate "labor conditions detrimental to the maintenance of the minimum standards of living necessary for health, efficiency and well-being of workers."

The act established a maximum of forty-four working hours a week for the first year, forty-two for the next, and forty thereafter. Similarly, minimum wages of twenty-five cents per hour for the first year, thirty for the second, and forty for the ensuing six years were decreed. Employees were entitled to time-and-a-half pay if they worked overtime.

A Wages and Hour Division was set up in the Department of Labor and provision was made for the administrator of the new division to appoint committees to determine proper rates of pay for various industries. The act has been amended several times to increase minimum wages. In 1972 the minimum wage was $1.60.

FEATHERBEDDING

The word featherbedding is said to have originated in the railroad industry when some trainmen complained about the condition of the mattresses in their caboose. Upon learning that they found the corn husks, corn cobs, and cottonseed hulls uncomfortable, the irate trainmaster asked: "What do you brakemen want—feather beds?"

This term now applies to those work rules which require the employment of more workers than needed for the job. In addition, when technological advances eliminate positions, unions often insist that the workers be retained and receive their regular pay for doing nothing.

In 1963, when the Supreme Court ruled that railroads could modernize their work rules and eliminate many unnecessary jobs, the annual cost of featherbedding in national railroad contracts saddled our nation's carriers with an estimated $592,000,000. The Supreme Court decision did not affect state laws, many of which still call for featherbedding procedures. Other industries have been plagued with featherbedding but the practice appears to be gradually disappearing.

FOSTER, WILLIAM ZEBULON

This American Communist Party leader was born in Taunton, Massachusetts, on February 25, 1881. The family subsequently moved to Philadelphia where Foster was compelled to start work at age ten. As he traveled about, he observed the horrible working conditions which still existed in many places and whenever possible urged his fellow workingmen to organize.

At one point Foster was a follower of William Jennings Bryan,* then became a left-wing Socialist and joined the Industrial Workers of the World (IWW) in 1909. Two years later, while traveling through Europe as a correspondent for the IWW, he changed his mind again. Instead of backing a radical union which would compete with the older trade unions, he decided that the IWW should become a propaganda organization which would start "boring from within."

During World War I Foster appeared to sever his radical connections so that he could work for the government's Liberty Bond Drive. His performance was so impressive that when the AFL sought someone to organize the steel industry in 1918 Foster seemed the best candidate.

In 1921 Foster became general secretary of the newly founded Communist Party in the United States and ran on the party's Presidential ticket in 1924, 1928, and 1932. In 1930 Earl Browder took his post, but after Browder's

* Famous orator, lawyer, and political leader (1860–1925), was a Congressman and Democratic nominee for President in 1896, 1900, 1908.

expulsion from the party in 1945, Foster regained his former position. He was indicted in 1948 on charges of conspiracy to teach and advocate the overthrow of government by force, but was never brought to trial because of poor health. After he, too, was expelled from his Communist Party post in 1957, he moved to Russia and continued to write for Communist publications until his death in Moscow on September 1, 1961.

(See also: Communists in the Labor Movement; Steel Strikes.)

FRANKENSTEEN, RICHARD T.

A union organizer who was once described as a "raucous, fleshy ex-football tackle." He was a member of the early Automotive Industrial Workers Association and was identified with the Communist movement. In May, 1936, on the advice of Father Charles E. Coughlin (the "Radio Priest" who advocated social changes), Frankensteen joined the United Automobile Workers (UAW) which had been formed in August, 1935. While working in the Dodge automobile plant he became the chief union organizer in the factory.

After General Motors and Chrysler workers had been organized, Walter Reuther and Frankensteen led the UAW organizers against the Ford Motor Company. On May 26, 1937, at the "Battle of the Overpass," they learned the cruel nature of their adversary.

(See also: "Battle of the Overpass"; Walter Reuther; United Automobile Workers.)

FRICK, HENRY CLAY

This industrialist was born in West Overton, Pennsylvania on December 19, 1849. After limited schooling, he clerked in his uncle's store at age sixteen and invested his earnings in the Connellsville coal district where one of the richest veins of coal had been discovered. At age twenty-two, he borrowed money from Judge Thomas Mellon of Pittsburgh to organize the Frick Coke Company. The demand for coke soon grew, and by the time he was thirty, Frick was the "coke king" and a millionaire.

Andrew Carnegie, head of Carnegie Steel, was impressed by Frick's business ability and became the largest single stockholder in the coke company, a position which assured his own firm a guaranteed supply of fuel for its furnaces. Carnegie then made Frick chairman of the board of Carnegie Steel, a post the younger man held for eleven years. During this time Frick improved the company administration, bought out several competitors, and purchased a large iron reserve in the Minnesota Mesabi range.

Frick's name became associated with the Homestead Strike of 1892. Although Carnegie agreed that Frick must break the strike at the Homestead, Pennsylvania mill, he did not approve of hiring Pinkerton strikebreakers and the resulting bloodshed. At first public opinion went against Frick, but after Alexander Berkman, an anarchist, tried to kill him, sympathy for the industrialist became evident.

After Frick and Carnegie quarreled in 1899. Frick left the company and started the United States Steel Corporation, then bought out Carnegie Steel two years later. Frick died in New York City on December 2, 1919.

Today many people know of Frick only because of the 150 acre park he left to the city of Pittsburgh, and for his home in New York City which contains the Frick collection of priceless art. After Mrs. Frick's death in 1935, the home was opened to the public as a museum and more than 200,000 people visit it annually.

(See also: Homestead Strike.)

FRINGE BENEFITS

This term refers to benefits an employer gives his workers in addition to wages. These may include paid holidays, paid vacations, pensions, life, accident and health insurance, medical examinations, free lunches and/or coffee breaks, tuition for evening courses, free transportation in the company's busses, trains, or planes, discounts on purchases of company products, free uniforms, bonuses, profit sharing, stock purchase plans, incentive pay plans, wash-up time, travel time, etc.

Frequently unions agree to accept additional fringe benefits in place of wage increases because many fringe benefits are not taxed, whereas extra pay is subject to income, and in some cases, social security taxes.

FULL EMPLOYMENT ACT OF 1946

In order to forestall any chance of a postwar depression, Congress adopted a bill known as the Full Employment Act of 1946 which stated that hereafter the federal government would be responsible for the nation's economic growth and stability.

The act established a Congressional Joint Committee on the Economic Report made up of seven Senators and an equal number of Representatives. The law required the committee to evaluate the President's annual Economic Report and propose stabilization measures.

In addition, Section 2 of the Act stated: "It is the continuing policy and responsibility of the federal government . . . to promote maximum employment, production and purchasing power." To accomplish this goal, the law established the Council of Economic Advisers * with the following duties: to analyze the national economy and its various segments; to advise the President on economic developments; to appraise the economic programs and policies of the federal government; to recommend to the President policies for economic growth and stability; to assist in the preparation of economic reports of the President to the Congress.

After the Congress has received and considered the President's annual economic report it may adopt such legislation as is desirable or required.

* Early in 1972 President Nixon appointed Mrs. Marina Whitman, economics professor at the University of Pittsburgh, to the Council. This appointment made Mrs. Whitman one of the Administrations's highest ranking women appointees.

GENERAL MANAGERS' ASSOCIATION

The General Managers' Association was a voluntary semi-secret society of some twenty-four railroads serving Chicago during the 1890's.

In March, 1893, the Association established the "Chicago scale" of pay for switchmen and in August announced a general wage reduction to "equalize" pay on all member railroads at the lowest possible levels. At the same time, all other railroads which did not serve Chicago were invited to join and soon some fifty-eight roads were members. The principal reason for broadening the membership was to obtain added strength to fight and destroy the American Railway Union (ARU) which Eugene V. Debs had formed that year.

The following year when the Pullman Company was struck by its employees and members of the ARU refused to handle its cars, the General Managers' Association voted to help Pullman. The chairman stated their real goal when he said: "We can handle the railway brotherhoods but we cannot handle the ARU . . . We cannot handle Debs. We have got to wipe him out."

After riots, bloodshed, and the subsequent collapse of the strike, President Grover Cleveland appointed an investigatory commission which, among other indictments, severely criticized the General Managers' Association as an illegal organization that had been established to evade the anti-trust law.

(See also: Eugene V. Debs; Pullman Strike.)

GOLDBERG, ARTHUR JOSEPH

The son of poor Russian immigrants, this lawyer and public official was born on August 8, 1908, on Chicago's West Side. His father died when he was three, and by the time he was twelve Goldberg was earning money as a delivery boy. He worked his way through Northwestern University, obtaining his doctorate in law in 1930. His own law office opened in Chicago during 1933 and he served as counsel for many of the largest unions. Appointed general counsel of the CIO and United Steelworkers in 1948, Goldberg helped the CIO expel its communist sympathizers. Goldberg also was one of those who were instrumental in bringing about the AFL-CIO merger in 1955. Thereafter, as special counsel to the AFL-CIO, he drafted the federation's ethical practices code and acted in a liaison capacity between his client and the government.

On January 21, 1961, President John F. Kennedy appointed Goldberg his first Secretary of Labor and the following year named him an associate justice of the Supreme Court. President Lyndon B. Johnson persuaded Goldberg to resign from the court to become the chief American representative to the United Nations. After Goldberg left this post he returned to private practice and became a partner in a New York City law firm.

GOMPERS, SAMUEL

This famous labor leader was born in England, January 27, 1850. He lived in the London Spitalfields slum and attended the Jewish free school there, but because the family was so poor, his father apprenticed him to a shoemaker when he was ten. This trade was not to his liking so he became a carpenter's apprentice, at the same time attending night school and involving himself in neighborhood activities. When young Gompers was thirteen, his family emigrated to America; the following year he joined the cigar maker's union. When he obtained a job in a cigar making factory, he became active in union affairs and as spokesman for his associates won them many concessions.

In 1875 Adolph Strasser, the aggressive president of the Cigar Makers' International Union, joined him in forming the largest affiliate, Local 144. Gompers was elected president of the local three years later and merged his local into the Cigar Makers' International and instituted reforms that included uniform initiation dues, central control over strikes, equalization of funds among various locals, and the establishment of a strike fund. This enlightened leadership attracted fifteen thousand new members and although the union lost its first strike, it managed to feed the membership and gained invaluable experience. After the strike Gompers was blacklisted, whereupon he threw himself into the trade union movement to concentrate his attention on the national labor movement.

In 1881, as a union delegate, he attended a meeting called in Pittsburgh to consider the creation of a new national organization which was named the Federation of Organized Trades and Labor Unions of the United States and Canada. Since it lacked a central headquarters, issued no charters and received no dues, the organization was weak and ineffective. Nevertheless, delegates met annually, and in 1884 one of the resolutions they adopted provided "that eight hours shall constitute a legal day's work from and after May 1, 1886." This provocative proclamation brought many recruits to the union, especially trade union Knights, because Terence Powderly opposed the short workday. Although thousands struck on May 1 for a shorter workday, the strategy failed and few won the concession. Undaunted, Gompers seized the opportunity to capitalize on the troubles besetting the Knights after the collapse of the southwestern railroad strike and the Haymarket Riot. On December 8 of that same year, a meeting was held at which the American Federation of Labor was formed, with Gompers its first president at an annual salary of one thousand dollars.

The organization of the new AFL was based on the principal of craft autonomy—each organized craft to have its own constitution, rules and procedures for dealing with employers—rather than one big union with mixed assemblies made up of skilled and unskilled workers. For the next fifty years the AFL was to be the dominant, and sometimes the only, representative for organized craft workers. A good part of its success stemmed from Gompers' insistence on working for economic gains through collective bargaining with employers rather than engaging in political action, an activity which up to that time had usually proved disastrous to each new labor movement.

Gompers continued as president of the AFL (except for one year) until his death December 13, 1924. A tireless worker, who in his later years associated freely with presidents, congressmen and Wall Street bankers, he nevertheless kept close to the rank and file workers, with whom he was proud to be associated. Ambitious, honest, always ready to make any personal sacrifice for labor's cause, and one who sought neither personal gain nor political favor, he died a poor man.

Gompers believed in the permanence of capitalism and the need for trade unions to work with, not against, the system. He feared that intellectuals and socialists, if admitted to unions, would lead trade unionism astray. He saw the importance of craft unionism for skilled workers and the need to win higher wages, shorter hours, and better working conditions for them. At the same time he opposed labor's involvement in politics lest this destroy union solidarity and give the socialists opportunity to take over the movement. Because he thought that unskilled labor was the natural enemy of the craftsman, he opposed industrial unionism, an issue which did not split the AFL until thirteen years after his death.

In his autobiography he stated: ". . . and I rejoice in the conviction that the bona fide trade union movement is the one great agency of the toiling masses to secure for them a better and higher standard of life and work."

GREEN, WILLIAM

This well-known AFL leader was born in Coshocton, Ohio, on March 3, 1873. When he was fourteen, he left school to work on a railroad gang as a water boy for fifty cents a week. At sixteen he apprenticed in a coal mine and thereafter became interested in the labor movement. He was only eighteen when he was elected secretary of his local union, twenty-seven when he advanced to the presidency of the Ohio Subdistrict of the United Mine Workers (UMW), and thirty-three when he become president of the Ohio district organization.

Green served two terms in the Ohio Senate and helped achieve passage of a workmen's compensation bill. At the same time he held the office of Secretary-Treasurer of the UMW and in 1913 also became a member of the AFL's executive council when John P. White, president of the UMW, refused the position as beneath his dignity. Green gradually worked his way up in the AFL and by 1924 was third vice-president. Late that year, thanks to the backing of his chief, John L. Lewis, he was elected president after Samuel Gompers died. Among labor leaders Green stood out as a man of exceptional character. The father of five daughters and one son, he did not smoke, drink, swear or gamble, a rare combination in any man! Under Green's direction the AFL membership grew steadily and won widespread public respect for the labor movement.

Although Lewis had been one of Green's most loyal supporters, he later split the AFL when he and Green disagreed over industrial versus craft unionism. In 1937 Lewis took eight of the largest unions out of the AFL into the CIO.

During World War II Green did much to work out the labor movement's "no strike pledge." Although greatly opposed to the National Labor Relations Board, he pledged his cooperation and promised to halt his feuding with the CIO for the duration of the war.

Green's greatest ambition was to bring the CIO back into the ranks of the AFL. He died in his home town on November 21, 1952, without realizing his goal, just three years before the AFL-CIO merger.

GUARANTEED ANNUAL WAGE

This is an agreement wherein an employer promises to pay his workers all or part of their regular wages even if the plant is closed.

The Bureau of Labor Statistics conducted a study of this revolutionary concept in 1945–46 and defined the term to mean guaranteed employment of at least three months each year or payment of an equal amount of wages. Since then a number of such plans were adopted with different types of coverage but the idea received its first real publicity in 1955 when Walter Reuther, president of the United Auto Workers (UAW), wrote in *Fortune* magazine that he did not consider the guaranteed annual wage (or guaranteed annual employment as it is sometimes called) the answer to all of our industrial relations problems. He did state, however, that it might become "an important lever for raising the sights of business leadership so that their planning takes into account the needs of the workers in their plants and of the entire community for a steady flow of income and purchasing power."

The automobile industry raised few objections to the idea and in June 1955 the UAW signed an agreement with the Ford Motor Company whereby the corporation set up a trust fund to total $55,000,000 within three years. It would be used to supplement unemployment insurance for workers who were laid off by making payments for twenty-six weeks on the basis of 65 percent of take home pay for the first four weeks, and 60 percent for the next twenty-two weeks. General Motors Corporation signed a similar contract with the UAW.

The term *guaranteed annual wage* should not be confused with the term *guaranteed income* which refers to one possible solution to the poverty problem. Guaranteed income would give unemployed, part-time workers, or those paid sub-standard wages a minimum income-floor for every family.

GUFFEY-SNYDER COAL ACT

This law, officially known as the Bituminous Coal Conservation Act of 1935 (and sometimes called the "Little NRA"), established a National Bituminous Coal Commission to stabilize conditions in the coal industry. The act guaranteed labor the right to bargain collectively and established rules for wages and working conditions. It also provided for a code of minimum and maximum prices.

The following year in the case of *Carter v. Carter Coal Company,* the Supreme Court invalidated the act because the labor provisions were deemed unconstitutional delegation of legislative powers.

H

HARD CORE UNEMPLOYED

This term refers to those who can and are willing to work but are unable to obtain employment even during periods when labor is in short supply. The hard core is usually unemployable because of mental or physical handicaps, lack of education or suitable skills, inability to relocate, or lack of information about the job market.

HAYMARKET RIOT

The Haymarket Riot was one of the most famous of the nineteenth century although it was not the bloodiest. A meeting had been called in Chicago's Haymarket Square by the International Working People's Association to protest the brutal and unnecessary police killing of four strikers and the wounding of others at the McCormick factory the previous day. On the night of May 4, 1886, some 250 men had gathered about a wagon where Samuel Fielden, an anarchist, was speaking about the insecurity of the laboring man and the problems he faced.

"In conclusion. . . ." He was about to end his speech when 180 policemen appeared in front of the wagon and the captain ordered the crowd to disperse peacefully.

"We are peaceable," Fielden insisted, as he and the other speakers jumped off the wagon. An instant later an explosion close to the first line of patrolmen killed a Sergeant Degan and knocked down six other policemen. After a few seconds of quiet, the uninjured police charged

84

at the fleeing crowd. A minute later the Haymarket Riot was over. Ten were dead, fifty injured.

"Hang them first and try them afterward," many urged when they read about the riot. Fielden and six allegedly innocent companions received the death sentence. Four were executed, one committed suicide, two received long sentences but later were granted unconditional pardon. This riot capped years of labor violence and strikes and from all sides there were demands that something be done to stop the waves of lawlessness.

After the Haymarket Riot, *John Swinton's Paper,* published in New York, stated that the bomb "was a godsend to the enemies of the labor movement. They have used it as an explosive against all the objects that the working people are bent on accomplishing, and in defense of all the evils that capital is bent upon maintaining."

A nine-foot statue of a nineteenth century policeman commanding peace with an upraised arm was erected in Haymarket Square in 1889. Since that time, it has been the target of vandals and bombs in 1969 and 1970. After the second attack, the statue was placed under twenty-four hour police guard and Haymarket Square was watched by a hidden television camera. In 1972 the statue was moved to the lobby of Police Headquarters for economy reasons. (See also: Anarcho-Syndicalism.)

HAYWOOD, WILLIAM DUDLEY

William Dudley Haywood was born in Salt Lake City, Utah, on February 4, 1869. From the time he was a young boy, he worked in and around mines and became active in the affairs of the Western Federation of Miners which was formed in 1893. In 1904 he took part in the violent strike at Cripple Creek, Colorado, where the governor declared martial law after an antiunion mob went on a rampage, killing five men and burning the union hall.

The turbulent labor movement in the west apparently appealed to "Big Bill," a tall, burly man, blind in one eye, and capable of providing leadership for the frontiersmen type of worker. Many felt that Haywood's kind of unionism was bred in the rough mining camps of the west. He was one of the early advocates of industrial unionism, organizing the unskilled, and using direct militant action to achieve their goals.

A year after the Cripple Creek strike, Haywood addressed a convention called by the Western Labor Union in Chicago. "Fellow workers," he shouted, "this is the Continental Congress of the Working Class. . . . The aims and objects of this organization shall be to put the working class in possession of the economic power, the means of life, in control of the machinery of production and distribution, without regard to capitalist masters." A few days later, under the direction of Haywood, Eugene V. Debs and Daniel De Leon, the Industrial Workers of the World (IWW) was born.

During the following year Haywood was falsely charged with the murder of the former governor of Idaho. After a well publicized trial at which the famous lawyer, Clarence Darrow, defended them, Haywood and three others were acquitted.

In 1912 Haywood, who had been a member of the Socialist Party since 1901, was expelled with other IWW members for advocating "violence, sabotage and crime." That same year Haywood led the IWW strike against the American Woolen Company in Lawrence, Massachusetts, a confrontation which ended in a major victory for the IWW and gave it national prominence. This was the high point for Haywood and the IWW. In 1913 the union lost an important strike in Paterson, New Jersey, and thereafter the union's popularity quickly dropped. Haywood and the other leaders came out against the European war and later opposed America's entry into World War I. "Big Bill" was indicted along with 165 other IWW leaders and convicted of sedition and sentenced to twenty years in prison. Haywood appealed, was released, and while awaiting a new trial jumped bail in 1921 and fled to Russia where he died on May 18, 1928.

(See also: Industrial Workers of the World; Lawrence Textile Strike; Paterson Silk Strike.)

HERRIN MASSACRE

Early in 1922 when John L. Lewis of the United Mine Workers (UMW) started negotiating for a new contract covering the region from Pennsylvania to Illinois, the mine operators refused to bargain for the whole area as Lewis had requested. Instead, they insisted on hammering out contracts district by district since this would be more to their advantage. As a result miners were called off their jobs and started picketing. This activity was peaceful everywhere except in the Connellsville, Illinois region.

On June 21 the Southern Illinois Coal Company, which had previously recognized the UMW, hired men from another union. The regular miners tried to talk with the strikebreakers but two were killed by machine guns when they approached the mine. The company erected a stockade about the area and brought in Hargreaves Secret Service operatives from Chicago to guard their property.

Tension mounted quickly in Herrin and other towns. Mobs broke into stores to seize all available arms and then surrounded the stockade. When the guards fired at them, they returned shots and prepared to storm the fence. A truce was arranged which provided that the guards and strikebreakers could leave the mine safely if they returned home.

As the guards, mine managers, and strikebreakers walked away from the stockade, they were attacked by some of the strikers who were crazed with fury and a desire for revenge. Nineteen strikebreakers and two strikers were murdered and many were injured. President Warren Harding immediately denounced the killings and bolstered the fight for open shops by saying: "A free American has the right to labor without any other's leave." Subsequently all of the miners accused of the murders were exonerated by a sympathetic jury.

The massacre proved disastrous to the UMW. Miners in Alabama, Colorado, Maryland, western Pennsylvania, Texas, Virginia, West Virginia, and Utah deserted the union. The only new contracts Lewis signed were in Illinois, Indiana, and Ohio.

HILLMAN, SYDNEY

This labor leader was born in Zagare, Lithuania in 1887. Sent to the town's Talmudic seminary at the age of twelve, the boy became interested in science and at fifteen was employed as a laboratory assistant in a chemical plant.

During the revolution of 1905, he joined the Lithuanian underground trade union movement, and when he was twenty came to Chicago where he found a job as apprentice cutter in the clothing factory of Hart, Schaffner and Marx. A twelve-hour day earned him seven dollars a week, but did not leave him too tired to study economics and English during the evening at Hull House.

Soon Hillman's fellow workers, most of whom were earning only two to four dollars a week for sixty to sixty-four hours' work, considered him an authority on labor matters and looked to him for leadership. In 1910 he organized a strike of pressers, tailors, trimmers, and spongers, but because the various ethnic groups distrusted each other, the strike failed. The following January the rank and file asked him to represent them and set up a procedure to settle their grievances. Three years later he was elected president of the newly organized Amalgamated Clothing Workers, remaining as its head until his death in 1946.

Hillman stressed the need to unionize workers in mass production industries rather than by crafts. At the same time he believed that a union had a responsibility to assist the clothing manufacturers.

"We help the employer for one excellent reason," he said in 1923. "The clothing workers must make their living out of the clothing industry—just like their employers." The Amalgamated worked closely with and cooperated with employers, lending them money and undertaking costly and valuable research from time to time. For its members the union offered cooperative banking, housing, and social security programs. This enlightened program was brought to Franklin D. Roosevelt's attention and he later became a close friend of Hillman's.

Hillman founded the American Labor Party in 1936 to back Roosevelt for reelection and subsequently served as acting chairman of the organization. He worked closely with John L. Lewis in forming the CIO and kept a close watch on the union's progress. He also formed the Textile Workers Organizing Committee which signed up 400,000 workers during 1937.

During World War II Hillman headed the labor section of the Office of Production Management and was vice-chairman of the War Production Board for three years. In 1943 he established the CIO's Political Action Committee to support President Roosevelt's bid for a fourth term. This led to publication of a pamphlet which told labor chiefs and Democratic Party workers how to plan and run political campaigns. At the Democratic Convention of 1944 President Roosevelt instructed his manager that party platform plans and strategy must be "cleared with Hillman." "Clear it with Sydney" became a slogan of Republican opponents who objected to the activities of this union political machine which Hillman had created.

Following the war Hillman attended labor meetings in Europe and served as vice-president of the World Federation of Trade Unions. He died July 10, 1946 at Point Lookout, New York.

(See also: American Labor Party; Congress of Industrial Organizations.)

HOFFA, JAMES RIDDLE

James Riddle Hoffa, who became leader of the Teamsters' Union, was born February 14, 1913, in Brazil, Indiana. His father, a coal driller, died when he was seven, and Jimmy was forced to leave school after finishing seventh grade in order to help support the family. When seventeen, Hoffa, a chunky young man, was a platform loader in a Detroit bakery where he organized his associates into a union and obtained a Teamsters' charter. Two years later he sought the presidency of the Detroit Joint Teamsters' Council. He received only four of the twenty council delegates' votes but nevertheless proclaimed himself president. "I just walked in and took over," he said.

He next founded a state-wide Teamster Conference and advanced to the post of state Teamster boss. Then he moved in on businessmen. When he was twenty-seven, he was indicted by the federal government for conniving with waste paper collecting companies to establish a monopoly. For this he received a one thousand dollar fine.

By 1952 he was so powerful that he obtained the presidency of the Teamsters' Union for Dave Beck and the vice-presidency for himself and became leader of two of its four regional conferences. He helped elect judges, contributed generously to various political campaigns, and even ran his own man for lieutenant governor. Those planning to get into labor racketeering and needing union charters, sought his help. The AFL-CIO, after examining his record, condemned his underworld associates.

In 1957 the McClellan Committee listed eighty-two charges against Hoffa, accusations that ranged from using terror against members and protecting rackets, to accepting favors from employers and harboring criminals. When Dave Beck was sent to prison and therefore had to step down as president of the Teamsters, Hoffa immediately declared himself a candidate for the post. The union elected him president, whereupon the Teamsters were thrown out of the AFL-CIO.

Meanwhile, Hoffa was indicted for wiretapping and perjury, but he fought back savagely with every possible legal device, even suing Senator Robert Kennedy and others for libel. The court appointed a board of monitors to supervise the union's conduct of its affairs. Although convicted on various counts Hoffa did not go to jail until 1967 and was set free less than five years later under a conditional commutation of sentence in which President Nixon specified he cannot "engage in the direct or indirect management of any labor organization" until March 6, 1980.

THE HOMESTEAD STRIKE

In 1892 the skilled steelworkers who belonged to the Amalgamated Association of Iron, Steel and Tin Workers had agreed not to accept wage cuts at the Homestead plant of the Carnegie Steel Company. They walked off their jobs and were followed by the unorganized workers, whereupon Henry Clay Frick, the company's manager, closed the plant and erected a high fence topped with barbed wire around the mills. Then Frick hired three hundred Pinkerton detectives to guard the plant and enable him to import strikebreakers.

On the night of July 5, 1892, two barges carrying the armed detectives were towed up the Ohio and Monongahela Rivers to the Carnegie property, situated opposite the southeastern part of Pittsburgh. When the barges approached the Carnegie Mills about 4 a.m., the strikers, who knew about Frick's plan, opened up with gunfire hoping to drive the Pinkertons away. For the next twelve hours shots were exchanged by the two "armies." Finally, the strikers set fire to barrels of oil which they had emptied onto the water. This trapped the detectives who were now jammed into one barge but had no tug to pull them to safety.

The Pinkertons ran up a white flag and agreed to discard their arms and ammunition in return for a guarantee of safe conduct out of town. When they came ashore, however, they were forced to run through the frenzied mob of strikers and sympathizers who attacked them with stones and clubs before they reached a train that was waiting to take them to Pittsburgh.

A week later eight thousand state militia arrived to declare martial law and open the plant to strikebreakers. The strike leaders were then charged with the murder of the Pinkertons killed in the July 5 battle and the mill resumed production. By November, when the union conceded defeat, two thousand strikebreakers were at work, and only eight hundred of the four thousand men who had gone out on strike were rehired.

Although some people condemned management for using a private army of Pinkertons whenever it wanted to crush a strike, others believed that a company had an obligation to work out a settlement with its employees. The prevailing belief at that time was that the company had the right to protect the strikebreakers it had hired and was therefore justified in its action. The Amalgamated union was smashed, and it was forty years before the steelworkers had another strong union of their own.

(See also: Henry Clay Frick; Pinkerton Agency.)

HUTCHESON, WILLIAM L.

This prominent labor leader and head of the carpenters' union was born in Saginaw, Michigan on February 7, 1874. His father, a ship's carpenter, taught him his trade. He joined the Brotherhood of Carpenters in 1902 and was elected second vice-president in 1912, vice-president the next year, and when the president died in 1915, automatically succeeded him.

Hutcheson is an example of a labor leader who acted like a czar. During his lifetime career as president of this union, he destroyed all rivals and made the Brotherhood one of the strongest organizations in the country. Described by *Time* magazine as "just as hard-boiled, almost as ambitious as John L. Lewis," he made many enemies in his union because of his allegedly illegal and dictatorial tactics to gain his objectives and keep control. More than once he was accused of making secret "sell-out" deals with employers.

William Hutcheson died October 20, 1953 and his son, Maurice A. Hutcheson took his place as president of the union.

(See also: United Brotherhood of Carpenters and Joiners of America.)

I •••

INDENTURED SERVANT

During the colonial period, especially during the 1600's and 1700's, many Europeans sold themselves into servitude in order to obtain the necessary passage to America. These redemptioners or free-willers agreed to sell their labor after reaching the colonies and thereby repay the cost of the ocean transportation.

INDUSTRIAL ALLIANCES

As part of the antilabor campaign which gained strength after 1900, Industrial Alliances of employers called a national convention in 1903 and established the Citizens' Industrial Association. Their purpose was to lobby and swing public opinion against labor so that the public would think of the closed shop as "Un-American."

In 1906 more than four hundred employers' associations sent delegates to another convention where the president, C. W. Post, reported that his group had discovered an enormous labor trust which was oppressing the workingman and the "common American citizen." Apparently the exact nature of the so-called labor trust was never revealed so it can only be surmised that Post meant the American Federation of Labor.

(See also: Antiunion Campaign.)

INDUSTRIAL BROTHERHOOD

This term refers to a secret society which was established by several national trade associations in July, 1873, to replace the defunct National Labor Union which collapsed after its membership had become divided three years earlier.

The new Industrial Brotherhood was pledged not to "deteriorate into a political party, or a refuge for played out politicians." Enthusiasm for the organization was sustained through the second annual membership meeting even though many members were unemployed due to the current depression. In 1875, when the third meeting was convened, the few members who attended were so discouraged that the society soon disappeared. All that survived were the preamble of their constitution and certain platform planks which the Knights of Labor later adopted.

(See also: National Labor Union.)

INDUSTRIAL DEMOCRACY

This term refers to the relationships which exist in a business or factory between management and labor. Before employers were legally compelled to recognize and deal with unions, an employee had no say regarding his working conditions and was at the mercy of arbitrary or autocratic decisions of the management without having any opportunity to present his grievances or problems for consideration.

Today, where a majority of employees in a plant vote to organize and bargain with the management, collective bargaining provides a democratic machinery for all workers to participate, express their views, and enjoy equal representation.

INDUSTRIAL REVOLUTION

This term refers to the transformation which took place in industry during the years between 1750 and 1850. It was the French economist, J. A. Blanqui (1798–1854), who referred to the changes which had recently taken place as the Industrial Revolution, but it was not a sudden event as is often thought. Instead, it was a long, evolutionary process.

In Europe four out of five workers were farmers in 1750. Then, gradual improvement in the production of goods caused major occupational shifts. The invention of the steam engine, the spinning and weaving machines, as well as improvements in iron making, paved the way for the factory system which took much of the handcrafting of goods out of the homes and into the newly built factories. All of the processes involved in making textiles, for example, had been carried on in homes, but gradually this work was shifted to the factory where machines took over much of the work. The spinning jenny which the English weaver, James Hargreaves, invented around 1764, produced a number of threads simultaneously, in contrast to the single thread which came from a spinning wheel.

Two years later, Richard Arkwright invented the water frame which was the first means of replacing hand power with water power. The steam engine, however, was probably the most important invention in speeding the industrialization of many countries. It enabled manufacturers to locate factories in or near cities where there were large labor forces rather than having to build them where water was available.

The early period of the Industrial Revolution brought widespread human misery and exploitation. Machines frequently mutilated workers, many of whom then became unemployable. The long hours, hard work and bad working conditions practically dehumanized the men, women and children who spent most of their waking hours at machines. The new villages that surrounded the smoking plants bred disease and squalor due to crowded living conditions and low wages. At the same time profits made the capitalists even more prosperous.

During the so-called second phase of the Industrial Revolution, which started around 1850, railroads were responsible for the continued industrial growth. They solved the problem of distributing the goods which were mass-produced and kept the factory system prospering. During the second hundred years, oil, electricity and later, atomic power gradually replaced steam as motive power; transportation embraced the automobile and airplane; methods of communicating broadened to include telephones, radio, television, and the use of satellites; the development of chemicals, light metals, computers, and other new products opened vast new industrial vistas; cooperative scientific research brought undreamed of advances in industry and gigantic corporate empires multiplied in many industries.

In the United States many of the evils of the industrial system had been exposed by the start of the twentieth century. Subsequently, government stepped in to regulate industry and helped to bring about social reforms in many areas. Thanks to the Industrial Revolution, the United States became the world's strongest and richest nation, but ironically, even in the 1970's, its people still have failed to solve some of the social problems which were set in motion when the Industrial Revolution first began.

Industrial Spying

Spying on employees reached its zenith during the middle 1930's when many corporations did their best to prevent the formation of labor unions and endeavored to discover and fire all workers who were trying to organize their employees. There was nothing new about this practice; it had been prevalent in one way or another since employers first opposed unions.

During the 1930's the American Plan became popular and employers' organizations worked to undermine unions. The National Metal Trades Association provided an example of how one such group allegedly served its membership. In addition to planting industrial spies in members' plants, whenever locals of the International Association of Machinists (IAM) went on strike, the National Metal Trades Association was ready to replace the union members with strikebreakers. As a result membership of the International Association of Machinists dropped from 330,800 in 1920 to 77,900 in 1924.

Private detective agencies' "detectives," were more often really strikebreakers who did a little spying. In 1936, the Senate's Civil Liberties Committee (better known as the La Follette Committee) investigated the nation's five largest detective agencies: Burns, Corporations Auxiliary Company, National Corporation Service, Pinkerton, and Railway Audit and Inspection. In addition, the Senators looked into the affairs of the Federal Laboratories, Lake Erie Chemical Co., and the Manville Manufacturing Co., major suppliers of tear and sickening gas, guns and ammunition. Other agencies were mentioned at the hearings as well as some 1,475 companies which were listed as their clients.

From January, 1933 to July, 1936, 282 corporations spent $9,440,132.15 on "labor relations"—not to aid unemployed workers or improve working conditions but to demoralize and destroy labor unions. They used strikebreakers and violence if necessary, and they employed industrial spies to watch fellow employees and report on their activities. The Pinkerton agency did a gross business of $2,300,000 in 1935 and had a thousand regular employees plus thousands of "contacts." Their clients included the largest and best known corporations in the country.

In correspondence advertising its products, the Manville Company said this about the effectiveness of its wares:

"Our equipment was used to break up the strike of the Ohio Rubber Co., at Willoughby, Ohio, and to break up the strike of the gear plant at Toledo, Ohio; was used at the Eaton Axle plant at Cleveland; at the Real Silk Hosiery Co. at Indianapolis; and at a great many small places. In each of the above cases, the equipment was used by the detective agencies brought in."

In its conclusions, the La Follette Committee stated: "The public cannot afford to let this challenge presented by industrial espionage go unnoticed. Through it, private corporations dominate their employees, deny them their constitutional rights, promote disorder and disharmony, and even set at naught the powers of the government itself."

(See also: American Plan; Pinkerton Agency.)

INDUSTRIAL UNION

An industrial union, also known as a vertical union, is one in which membership is open to all workers (skilled, semi-skilled, and unskilled) in a particular industry such as an automobile factory, a coal mine, a rubber plant, etc.

The first industrial unions appeared in the 1870's when the Knights of Labor was organized. Later, as the American Federation of Labor (AFL), the successor to the Knights, placed great emphasis on crafts, industrial unions tended to disappear. The AFL leadership was committed to affiliating only craft unions. The Industrial Workers of the World was an industrial union; when it died the Communist Party encouraged industrial unionism, but the movement never gained headway until the middle 1930's. At that time John L. Lewis, president of the United Mine Workers, organized the Committee on Industrial Organization (CIO) as part of the AFL. In 1937 the conservative leadership of the AFL evicted Lewis and the CIO, whereupon he started the Congress of Industrial Organizations as a rival and essentially an industrial union. The AFL and CIO merged in 1955.

(See also: American Federation of Labor; Congress of Industrial Organizations; Knights of Labor.)

INDUSTRIAL WORKERS OF THE WORLD

Delegates representing many unions and political groups attended a convention called by the Western Labor Union at Chicago in 1905. Among them were Eugene Debs, leader of the Socialist Party and William D. Haywood of the Western Federation of Miners. Haywood helped direct the deliberations in such a manner that the delegates finally agreed to establish a universal industrial union which would embrace all workers of the world. A platform for the new Industrial Workers of the World (IWW) declared in part:

"The working class and the employing class have nothing in common. Between these two classes a struggle must go on until the workers of the world organize as a class, take possession of the earth and the machinery of production and abolish the wage system. . . . It is the historic mission of the working class to do away with capitalism. . . . An injury to one is an injury to all."

The following year, the Western Federation of Miners, which had been responsible for founding the IWW, withdrew, leaving six thousand members. In no time this remnant split into two factions, those who vowed to overthrow capitalism through economic action that used strikes, sabotage, slowups, and violence, and those who thought the IWW should enter politics. The latter group resigned, whereupon the remaining Wobblies, or "I Won't Work," as IWW came to be called, recruited members among migratory harvest workers (mostly on the Pacific coast), lumbermen, western miners, and construction gangs. The leaders were tireless, going from strike to strike, helping organizers, manning picket lines, giving workers' families relief, all the while agitating and stirring up trouble. Although the word IWW became synonymous with violence, the union was genuinely interested in helping unskilled and unorganized workers.

The leadership knew how to create a feeling of solidarity and buck up members' morale. Their songs were sung lustily wherever members gathered, be it at harvest camps, union meetings or on picket lines. "The Red Flag," "Dump the Bosses Off Your Back," "Are You a Wobbly?" and "Hallelujah I'm a Bum!" were among the best known.

The IWW won its greatest victory at Lawrence, Massachusetts in 1912, but the following year it suffered a humiliating defeat in Paterson, New Jersey, an event which marked the beginning of its swift decline. When European hostilities broke out in 1914, the IWW took a stand against the war. The public labeled the union as pro-German and unpatriotic. As soon as the United States entered the war, government agents broke into all offices of the IWW and arrested its officers. Haywood and ninety-four others received jail sentences as high as twenty years. After the Communist Party was organized in the United States in 1919, most of the remaining Wobblies joined, and shortly thereafter the union was forgotten. In 1972 the IWW had about one thousand members, mostly young militants, many of them students.

(See also: William Dudley Haywood; Lawrence Textile Strike; Paterson Silk Strike.)

INFLATION

The term inflation usually refers to a period when prices climb because the supply of goods is not large enough to satisfy the public's purchasing power or demand. As prices rise during an inflationary period, money loses its value, companies may expand and earn larger profits and many people may have extra cash to spend. At the same time workers demand higher and higher wages to keep up with the inflated living costs. The increased wages, however, only add to the workers' purchasing power and raise prices again, thus creating an inflationary "wage-price spiral."

INJUNCTION

An injunction is a legal order issued by a court when the rights of a person or persons are threatened. The order can either prohibit a person, group or company from carrying out a given action, or can order that certain action be taken. Thus it was possible for an employer to go to a court and obtain an injunction forbidding a union to picket his plant, conduct a boycott, or undertake any other activities which he considered detrimental to his business.

In 1932 Congress passed the Norris-LaGuardia Act * which prohibited federal courts from issuing injunctions

---

* The legislation also outlawed use of employer "yellow-dog" contracts which the courts had supported since 1880. (See also: Yellow-dog Contracts.)

against labor unions unless certain procedures were followed. The union had to be given opportunity to state its case fully; there had to be proof that all possible efforts had been made to reach a peaceful settlement by mediation or other means; and it had to be shown that if no injunction were granted, more hardship would be caused one party than granting the injunction would cause the other.

The Taft-Hartley Act (1947) and amendments thereto, provided that injunctions may be issued in three different kinds of situations, the most important involving a national emergency strike. In the case of the Fair Labor Standards Act, the Secretary of Labor may seek injunctions to enforce the law's provisions.

(See also: Taft-Hartley Act.)

INTERNATIONAL LABOR ORGANIZATION

This agency was originally established in 1919 by the Versailles Peace Conference to engage in research in international labor and welfare matters in order to promote economic and social stability and improve living standards and labor conditions throughout the world. The United States did not join the International Labor Organization (ILO) until 1934 because of previous Congressional opposition to the League of Nations. In 1945 the ILO became an agency of the United Nations.

After George Meany, president of the AFL-CIO, accused the organization of becoming a sounding board for Soviet propaganda, Congress refused to pay the dues this country owed. The world labor body accomplished certain internal reforms and in 1970 won the Nobel Peace Prize. In 1972 President Richard Nixon warned that it is "not consistent with our national dignity to attempt to maintain influence and membership in the ILO if we are not prepared to pay our dues." Since Mr. Meany acknowledged that he now favored paying the twenty million dollars in back and current dues, it appeared that Congress might reinstate the United States as a full-fledged dues-paying member of the ILO.

INTERNATIONAL LADIES' GARMENT WORKERS' UNION

To understand the significance of this union, it is necessary to know that in the middle 1890's a wave of Russian, Romanian and Polish Jews came to New York. Most of them were skilled tailors and settled on the East Side of Manhattan where they entered the apparel trades. These trades were distinguished by offering the worst possible working conditions.

Employees were forced to work for as many as twelve hours a day, seven days a week, for four or five dollars. Tailors had to pay for their needles and thread and provide their own sewing machines. The doors were locked in the morning; no one might leave until night unless they became ill. Even toilets could not be used without special permission of the boss. Employers were famous for their chiseling and lack of ethics. From the beginning days of this industry, competition had been ruthless and harsh. Labor was so plentiful that a man who had fifty dollars to invest could start a business, hire people, and make them wait for their wages until he had sold the finished goods. Little wonder that starvation wages were the rule.

During the late 1800's numerous unions were organized among the oppressed garment workers, but most of the organizations lasted only a short time. In June, 1900, eleven delegates from seven union organizations, representing a total of two thousand members scattered among four cities, met to form the International Ladies' Garment Workers' Union (ILGWU). Little, if anything, of great importance was accomplished by the new group of workers until 1909, when the union conducted an unsuccessful strike of shirtwaist workers which was dubbed the "uprising of the 20,000." The women picketing in front of the shops were cruelly beaten by employers' hired thugs, and after two months the strike was canceled. It was not in vain, however, for the next year the union prepared more carefully for a walkout—called the "Great Revolt"—that involved some forty thousand cloak makers. This strike brought police brutalities against pickets; but the strikers won their dispute, and in September, 1910, a "Protocol of Peace" was signed. This was the new union's first real victory, and it brought tremendous improvements in working conditions to the long-oppressed garment workers.

Thereafter home work was abolished, workers did not have to pay for their needles, thread, or "fines." The normal workweek was six days with fifty-four hours. Ten holidays a year were granted, and those who wanted to observe the Jewish Sabbath on Saturday could have the option of working Sundays. Pay would be in cash, and piece workers would receive their money immediately instead of having to wait. A Joint Board of Sanitary Control, a Board of Arbitration, and a Committee of Grievances were also established.

Although the ILGWU made little progress expanding its membership during the next twenty years, it pioneered a number of "firsts" in the labor movement: the first union health center in 1913, the first vacation center in 1915, the first educational department for its employees in 1917, the first employer-contributed unemployment compensation plan in 1919.

Between 1920 and 1932, the union lost about three-quarters of its members as the Communists took over.

They believed that the union should help bring about the revolution in America and this alienated most of the members. When David Dubinsky was elected president and secretary-treasurer in 1932, the membership had fallen to about forty thousand. Under Dubinsky's leadership the union grew steadily and members enjoyed an ever-increasing number of benefits, thanks to his progressive ideas.

(See also: David Dubinsky.)

INTERNATIONAL LONGSHOREMEN'S ASSOCIATION

The International Longshoremen's Association (ILA), founded in 1892, made unfortunate headlines in 1953 because, among other things, it had been accused by the American Federation of Labor (AFL) of having close relationships with dock racketeers in New York City. At the AFL convention held that year, the Executive Council reported to the membership that "The ILA has permitted gangsters, racketeers and thugs to fasten themselves to the body of its organizations, infecting it with corruption and destroying its integrity, its effectiveness and its trade-union character. . . . For such, there is no place in the American Federation of Labor." An almost unanimous vote expelled the ILA.

The AFL then chartered a new union, the International Brotherhood of Longshoremen (IBL). At first the IBL met with success and within a year had enrolled some nine thousand members, but the real test came in New York City where the National Labor Relations Board (NLRB) conducted the elections to decide which union would represent the longshoremen. Seemingly the NLRB favored the ILA over the IBL. After two elections the NLRB announced victory for the ILA by 263 votes. The IBL lost a third election in 1956.

Meanwhile James Hoffa had promised to join the Teamsters with the ILA and lend their new ally $400,000. Although the Teamsters-ILA pact was dropped later, the IBL had been harmed to the point where the AFL-CIO * felt it could no longer afford to help the struggling union; the IBL gradually withdrew from the New York waterfront.

In 1959 George Meany was satisfied that the ILA had eliminated former abuses and recommended that the union be taken back into the AFL-CIO. The ILA was readmitted and subsequently merged the IBL into its membership.

IRON-CLAD OATHS

During the period, roughly, from the end of the Civil War until World War I, various employer associations advocated the use of many antiunion techniques. One of them was the "iron-clad oath" which referred to an employment contract in which the employee agreed not to join a union or encourage the formation of a union while working for the employer.

A typical iron-clad oath read: "I, the undersigned, in consideration of the John Doe Company giving me employment, do hereby agree with the said company to withdraw from any and all labor organizations during the time or term of employment with said company, and I further agree not to urge, request or try any means whatever to induce others to join such labor union or organization during same time."

(See also: Yellow-dog Contracts.)

* In 1955 the American Federation of Labor (AFL) and Congress of Industrial Organizations (CIO) had merged to form the AFL-CIO.

J ●●

JOURNAL OF UNITED LABOR

This journal was the official publication of the Knights of Labor which was organized in 1869 and had disintegrated by the end of the century.

JOURNEYMEN

A journeyman is a skilled tradesman or an artisan who has completed an organized and recognized apprenticeship program. During medieval times, a man who successfully completed his apprenticeship became a journeyman and was later admitted to the guild as a master who in turn might hire and train apprentices.

Today an apprenticeship program permits apprentices to study a trade while working and at the end of a certain period to qualify as a journeyman.

(See also: Apprenticeship.)

JOURNEYMEN SOCIETIES

In 1794, the Federal Society of Journeymen Cordwainers was established in Philadelphia and remained active until 1806. Considered the original "continuous organization" of workingmen, it has been called the nation's first trade union. Its membership was limited to journeymen shoemakers who, in the manner of later trade unionists, picketed their masters' shops when they went out on strike in 1799.

Shortly after the Philadelphia cordwainers started their organization, New York printers formed the first union in

that industry, and two years later the Journeymen Cabinet Makers established a society which was destined to last
for some time. Other groups of skilled workers organized
associations or trade societies. These were not unions as
we know them today but local associations restricted to
one craft.

The masters watched these first labor organizations
carefully and resisted having journeymen dictate what
wages should be paid as well as the terms of their working
conditions. Some masters went to court to stop this threat
to their independence. In Philadelphia a jury found six
members of the shoemaker unions guilty of going out on
strike for higher wages. Three years later, twenty-four
New Yorkers were fined for a criminal conspiracy involving a strike, and in 1815, an association of shoemakers was
indicted in Pittsburgh on similar grounds. It was not
until 1842 that a Massachusetts judge decided in the case
of *Commonwealth v. Hunt* that it was not illegal for a
union to strike for higher wages. Meanwhile, the early
journeymen societies had given way to national trade associations, the forerunner of which was the National Trades
Union established in 1834.

JURISDICTIONAL DISPUTES

In a jurisdictional strike, two unions disagree over
which should do a specific job or which should act as the
bargaining agent for a certain plant or company. During
the latter 1880's, the newly organized American Federation of Labor (AFL) and the well-established Knights of
Labor invaded each other's territory, encouraged workers
to revolt, and invited locals belonging to the other union
to switch into their own organization. Following the creation of the Congress of Industrial Organizations (CIO) in
1937, the AFL and CIO became involved in a tremendous

jurisdictional fight which involved almost every union in the country. CIO woodworkers fought AFL carpenters, CIO packinghouse workers raided the ranks of AFL meat-cutters, AFL paper mill workers opposed CIO paper workers. No union was safe from attack; only the railroad unions remained apart from the strife. It was the task of the National Labor Relations Board to settle which union was the proper bargaining agent where two or more claimed jurisdiction.

These jurisdictional conflicts often set off strikes and involved employers who were innocent victims and were subjected to serious financial loss. Eventually the public began to see itself as victimized by labor's irresponsibility and there was talk about wanting tough laws to regulate such labor practices. By 1940 four states had outlawed jurisdictional strikes, but with the advent of World War II these inter-union disputes disappeared.

KICKBACK

When a union official or a boss forces a worker to pay him part of his wages in order to obtain and/or hold his job, this practice is known as a kickback.

KNIGHTS OF LABOR

In 1868 some Philadelphia tailors under the leadership of Uriah S. Stephens, a Baptist minister, established the

Noble Order of the Knights of Labor. Stephens hoped to build a "giant brotherhood of toil" which would embrace all mankind. He did not believe in strikes or boycotts, and shortly after being elected Grand Master Workman in 1879, he resigned to enter politics. Terence V. Powderly took his place.

When organizing the Knights, Stephens had insisted that it be a secret fraternal society to protect the members from being fired or blacklisted for engaging in union activities. Only those who could give the correct passwords, pass grips, and countersigns might attend meetings so that "no spy of the boss can find his way into the lodge room to betray his fellows." It was not until 1881 that the name and activities of the organization were made public.

Anyone "working for wages or who at any time worked for wages" was eligible to join. The Knights advocated many social reforms including an eight-hour day, equal pay for equal work, abolishment of child labor, and establishment of cooperatives. After the original assembly of tailors was founded, a second assembly was formed of ship carpenters in 1872 and thereafter other local assemblies of carpenters, shoemakers, railroad men, miners, and craft workers were organized. As the movement spread, some assemblies signed up workers in many diverse trades, and if there were not enough men of one craft to justify an assembly, a mixed group was formed, often with unskilled workers. District assemblies of delegates from each of the local assemblies were provided, but it was not until 1878 that a National Assembly was set up as the top authority.

Under Powderly's leadership membership grew but fluctuated due to the failure of many strikes. After a strike had been called off, members were usually blacklisted, unable to obtain jobs, and therefore could not pay their dues. Unskilled workers were easily replaced by strike-

111

breakers and the Knights were seldom successful in conducting strikes for their craftsmen. In 1885 the union achieved its greatest victory when shopmen in railroads owned by Jay Gould went on strike in the southwest. For the first time, labor forced management of a large company to negotiate an agreement on its terms. Workingmen all over the country then rushed to join the Knights, pushing the membership up from 80,000 in 1885 to 700,000 a year later.

The tide turned quickly, however. The year 1886 proved disastrous for Powderly. The Knights lost their second strike against Gould's railroads. Powderly refused to support the eight-hour movement, and he turned his back on the Haymarket anarchists when they were on trial for their lives. As a result, membership dropped to less than seventy-five thousand by 1893, and that same year Powderly was replaced as Grand Master Workman by James R. Sovereign, an Iowa farm editor. Soon the Knights abandoned their original purpose and stated their aims as adjusting "natural resources and productive facilities to the common interests of the whole people." Their entrance into politics was unsuccessful and by 1900 the organization was practically extinct.

Although the newer American Federation of Labor was destined to become the overall leader of the union movement, the Knights played an important part in promoting unity among workingmen and helping them win social reforms. The Knights were also responsible for encouraging industrial unionism rather than restricting their membership to crafts as the AFL did originally. Thus it proved the forerunner of an important development in trade unionism which did not come about until the 1930's when industrial unions were established by the Committee for

Industrial Organization (later renamed the Congress of Industrial Organizations).

(See also: American Federation of Labor; Congress of Industrial Organizations; Terence V. Powderly.)

KOHLER STRIKE

Although it did not threaten the national security or public welfare, the Kohler strike attracted nationwide attention because of the "Don't Buy Kohler" campaign sponsored by the United Automobile Workers (UAW) and the fact that it became one of the longest strikes on record.

The Kohler Company, located in Sheboygan, Wisconsin, was founded in 1912 by John Michael Kohler who built a model town complete with recreation areas and community buildings for his employees. During the depression of the 1930's, Kohler kept production at capacity and stockpiled bathtubs at a loss of a million dollars a year. It was a highly paternalistic firm that felt responsible for its workers' welfare, but to many employees it was a "feudal system" which used labor spies and forbade any union activity.

Eventually the employees were organized and in 1952 the UAW signed up a majority of the production workers. Two years later, when the UAW demanded, among other things, a twenty cents an hour raise, a union shop, promotion according to seniority, and a company-financed pension plan, the company president, Herbert Kohler, refused, declaring that the real issue was whether Kohler or the union would run the company.

Kohler promised that all newly hired employees would not be laid off to make way for strikers who later wanted to return. For its part the union promised that when the strike was settled every striker would be reinstated. The UAW called a work stoppage on April 5, 1954, and in violation of federal and state laws, surrounded the plant with a mass picket line, reinforced with men brought in from outside, many of whom were said to have been hoodlums and even fugitives from the law. For fifty-four days production was halted, then the picket line was reduced to twenty-five under threat of court action, and some 1,600 workers reclaimed their jobs while new employees filled positions of those who remained on strike.

More than eight hundred acts of violence and vandalism followed, and Kohler employees who were labeled as enemies of labor lived in terror for their lives. By the time the strike entered its third year in 1956, production at the plant had long been normal. The strike continued officially as union boycotts proved unsuccessful, the National Labor Relations Board (NLRB) held hearings from 1955–1959, and the Senate's McClellan Committee investigated the strike in 1958. In 1960 the NLRB ruled Kohler guilty of unfair labor practices under the Taft-Hartley Act, whereupon the company appealed to the Supreme Court and lost.

Finally, after eight-and-a-half years, Kohler and the UAW signed a contract on October 7, 1962. Although the union had spent twelve million dollars, it had not gained the wage increase or union shop which were two of the key issues.

L ••

LABOR DAY

Labor Day is observed as a national holiday in all states and territories of the United States. In 1882 Peter J. McGuire of New York City's Central Labor Union, which was affiliated with the Knights of Labor, introduced a resolution setting aside the first Monday in September in honor of all working men and women. The first Labor Day parade was held in New York on September 5, 1882.

On February 21, 1887, the Oregon legislature declared Labor Day a legal holiday, designating the first Saturday in June for the observance. In 1893 the legislators changed the date to the first Monday in September, and the following June Congress passed a law naming the same date as a national holiday. It should be noted that Europeans have celebrated Labor Day on the first day of May since 1890.

LABOR FORCE

Each month the Bureau of Labor Statistics of the U.S. Department of Labor compiles figures to determine the number of people in the United States who are employed. The total is known as the labor force.

According to the Bureau of Labor Statistics: "This data is collected during the calendar week which includes the 12th of the month. Employed persons comprise all persons who, during that week, did any work for pay or profit, worked 15 hours or more as unpaid workers in a family enterprise, or did not work but had jobs or businesses from which they were temporarily absent for non-economic reasons. Unemployed persons comprise all persons not working during the survey week who had made specific efforts to find a job within the past 4 weeks and who were available for work, and persons who were on layoff from a job or waiting to report to a new wage or salary job within 30 days."

In January, 1972, the latest available date when this book went to press, the total labor force of the United States, including the Armed Forces, was 88,301,000 men and women. Of the civilian labor force which totaled 85,707,000, 3,393,000 were employed in agricultural jobs and 77,243,000 in non-agricultural positions. At that same time 5,071,000 persons were unemployed.

Distribution of the persons who were employed in non-agricultural positions was as follows: 26 percent in manufacturing, 22 percent in wholesale and retail trade, 19 percent in government, 17 percent in services, 6 percent in transportation and public utilities, 5 percent in finance, insurance, and real estate, 4 percent in contract construction, and 1 percent in mining. (Source: Monthly Labor Review, March, 1972.)

(See also: Unemployment.)

LABOR-MANAGEMENT RELATIONS

This term usually refers to the procedures which union representatives and managements have worked out to settle disputes. Most disagreements are resolved by negotiation or discussion. When this results in a written contract, it is called collective bargaining. On the other hand, labor management relations are often characterized by extreme measures such as lockouts, strikes, or even violence.

116

Labor-management relations are also referred to as industrial relations.

(See also: Arbitration; Collective Bargaining.)

Labor's Bill of Grievances

The rise of antiunionism at the turn of the century resulted in the defeat at the 1904 elections of many Congressmen friendly to labor. In 1906 delegates from some 118 international unions met in Washington, D.C. to discuss the use of more direct political pressure to combat the employers' antiunion campaign. This was unusual because the American Federation of Labor's (AFL) traditional non-political objectives had always dominated its policies.

The attendees drew up a paper which became known as "Labor's Bill of Grievances." It demanded an eight-hour law for all workingmen, total exclusion of Chinese laborers, legislation against using competitive convict labor, limits on immigration, elimination of injunctions in labor disputes, and exemption for unions from the antitrust laws.

Congress paid no attention to the Bill of Grievances, and the AFL's Executive Council voted to participate in the campaign of 1906. As a result, many of labor's enemies received smaller pluralities than usual and six AFL members were elected.

Again, following World War I when employers launched another antiunion campaign and sought to reestablish the open shop, the AFL found itself in a difficult position. The leaders were still reluctant to be drawn into direct political action. A meeting was called in December, 1919 and the delegates issued a new "Labor's Bill of Rights" which called for union recognition, a living wage, and prohibitions against the use of injunctions. The federation leaders refused to go beyond these demands and the union movement received no political assistance to help fight its enemies.

(See also: Antiunion Campaigns.)

LANDRUM-GRIFFIN ACT

Following the McClellan Hearings with their disclosures of violence and corruption in certain labor union tactics, Congress passed the Labor-Management Reporting and Disclosure Act of 1959, also known as the Landrum-Griffin Act after its sponsors in the House of Representatives. It was designed to eliminate improper activities by management and labor.

The law aimed to safeguard the interests of each union member by forcing union leadership to run the unions in a democratic manner. Officials who misused union funds would be fined and imprisoned. Communists and criminals who sought to serve as union officials could not be elected until five years after they had resigned their Communist membership or had been released from prison. The law also declared it a federal crime for anyone to interfere with the rights of a union member.

The act contains what has been called a "Bill of Rights" for labor because it (1) guarantees union members freedom of assembly and speech, control over union dues, fees and assessments, plus the right to sue their union and to protection against unwarranted disciplinary actions; (2) requires that reports be filed by union officers and employees as well as employers, and lists the records which unions and employers must keep and file with the Secretary of Labor; (3) regulates union elections, financial accounting, the qualifications of officers and employees; and (4) sets up penalties for embezzlement and making loans over two thousand dollars to union officers and employees.

Responsible union leadership could not object to these provisions of the law, but they were infuriated by the sections of the act which strengthened what union leaders considered the antilabor provisions of the Taft-Hartley Act. These pertained to secondary boycotts and the picketing of companies where another union was already recognized. The Landrum-Griffin Act also permitted the states to step into labor disputes if the National Labor Relations Board (NLRB) refused to do so. The Department of Labor administers all sections of the act except those which amend the Taft-Hartley Act, these portions being under the jurisdiction of the NLRB.

"The most severe setback in more than a decade," declared the Executive Committee of the AFL-CIO while the *Federationist* said the law's purpose was "to destroy labor." The act reflected the public's mistrust of union power and its fear of irresponsible leadership, but most people agreed that the law did not crush any of labor's real rights and that it was in the best interests of both labor and the public.

LAWRENCE TEXTILE STRIKE

On January 12, 1912, twenty thousand textile workers in the rambling mills at Lawrence, Massachusetts, went on strike. They were mostly Italians, Lithuanians, Poles, and Russians who worked long hours to make less than nine dollars a week. When the management cut their pay, the angry workers walked off their jobs. Some of the men and women belonged to the United Textile Workers (UTW), about a thousand had joined the radical Industrial Workers of the World (IWW), and the rest were unorganized.

Lawrence Textile Strike

As soon as the strike started, Joseph J. Ettor and Arturo Giovannitti, two leaders of the IWW, moved in to direct the strike. They arranged meetings of strikers, set up picket lines, and distributed relief to needy families. When the American Woolen Company tried to reopen the mills after refusing to talk with the IWW, there were clashes between police and strikers, and a woman was killed. Martial law was declared, Ettor and Giovannitti were arrested and accused of being responsible for the woman's murder.

"Big Bill" Haywood of the IWW rushed to Lawrence to take charge of the strike. Instead of advocating the usual violence which was part of the IWW tactics, he insisted on an attitude of passive resistance. As the strike continued, the problem of feeding the strikers' families became acute and sympathetic union members in other cities offered to take children of parents on strike. After several hundred children had been sent away, the president of the UTW accused the IWW of doing this to keep up the agitation and persuaded the authorities in Lawrence to announce that no more children could leave.

Defying the police order, Haywood prepared to send another group to Philadelphia. The children were brought to the station, lined up two by two, and were about to be marched to the train when the police ". . . closed in on us with their clubs, beating right and left, with no thought of the children who were in the most desperate danger of being trampled to death. The mothers and children were then rounded up and bodily dragged to a military truck and even then clubbed, irrespective of the cries of panic-stricken women and children . . ."—so stated the report of the Women's Committee of Philadelphia.

Protests poured in from every part of the country, and

although there were more arrests and attacks on strikers, the men and women stayed on the picket lines until March 12, when the American Woolen Company capitulated. A government report sums up the strikers' gains:

"Some thirty thousand textile mill employees in Lawrence secured an increase of wages of from five to twenty percent; increased compensation for overtime and reduction of the premium period from four weeks to two weeks. Also, in an indirect result of the Lawrence strike, material increases in wages were granted to thousands of employees in other textile mills throughout New England."

(See also: William Dudley Haywood; Industrial Workers of the World.)

LEWIS, JOHN LLEWELLYN

John Llewellyn Lewis was born February 12, 1880, at Lucas, Iowa. His father was a coal miner who knew what it meant to be blacklisted by the mine owners for having a union card. After attending elementary school young Lewis went to work and then entered the mines. When he turned twenty-one he began four years of travel through the west, working at many jobs, principally in mines. Then he returned to Lucas, married, and served as a delegate of a Lucas mine to the national convention of the United Mine Workers (UMW).

In 1909 he moved to Panama, Illinois, was elected president of the local union and became the union's state legislative representative in 1910. The following year Samuel Gompers, president of the American Federation of Labor (AFL), met him and was so favorably impressed that he hired Lewis as field representative of the AFL. In 1917 Lewis returned to the UMW as its statistician, then quickly rose to vice-president, acting president, and in 1920 its president.

Lewis became one of the most controversial labor leaders in the country as he led his miners through a succession of strikes to win better pay scales and improved working conditions. He was a hero to the UMW membership, but a long suffering public disliked him for his defiance of the government, his arrogance, his seeming unconcern for the general welfare, and the inconveniences his strikes caused whenever fuel was in short supply. Newspaper cartoonists exaggerated his huge bushy eyebrows and large head as they depicted him riding roughshod over the President and the government.

Aside from his activities as head of the UMW, Lewis is also remembered for his zeal in organizing production industries on a wide industrial rather than a narrow craft basis. In 1935 he was instrumental in forming within the AFL the Committee for Industrial Organization of which he became president. Two years later, when this group was expelled from the AFL, he changed the name to Congress of Industrial Organizations and continued as its president until 1940 when he resigned and concentrated his attention on running the UMW.

During World War II, Lewis' insolent and unpatriotic conduct was partly responsible for turning much of the public against labor and encouraging Congress to pass restrictive legislation which included the Smith-Connally Act (1943) and the Taft-Hartley Act (1947). In 1942 he quarreled with Philip Murray, the CIO president, and took his UMW out of that federation. Four years later, the AFL voted to readmit Lewis and the UMW, but the following year he withdrew * the UMW from the AFL and

---

* Lewis refused to sign the non-Communist oath which the Taft-Hartley Act required of all union officers although he never was a Communist and had opposed the Communist Party. His refusal to "grovel" and inciting of others to do the same in order to test the

his union continued its independence even after the AFL-CIO merger in 1955.

Lewis' final accomplishment was to establish the UMW's health and retirement programs. After he resigned as president of the union on January 14, 1960, he continued to serve as chairman of the union's welfare fund until his death in Washington, D.C. on June 11, 1969.

"LITTLE STEEL" FORMULA

Shortly after the United States became involved in World War II, President Franklin D. Roosevelt established a War Labor Board (WLB) consisting of twelve members equally divided among business, labor, and the public. In addition to other duties, the WLB was authorized to control hours of work and wages.

As spiraling prices pushed the cost of living higher and higher, unions petitioned for wage increases. At first the WLB considered each request on its own merit, but it soon was apparent that unless there were an overall program to stabilize the cost of goods and labor there would be runaway inflation.

In July, 1942, employees of the "Little Steel" companies * demanded an increase of a dollar a day. Hearings were held, and the WLB ruled that wage advances would be granted in amounts no greater than the cost of living increase that occurred between January, 1941, and May, 1942. Data prepared by the Bureau of Labor Statis-

law, led to a dispute within the AFL. In December, 1947, Lewis sent a note to President William Green which read: "We disaffiliate."

* The "Little Steel" companies included Bethlehem Steel Corp., Inland Steel Co., Republic Steel Corp., and Youngstown Sheet and Tube Co.

tics showed the cost of living increase to be 15 percent. When this amount was granted, the Little Steel workers received forty-four cents a day additional wages instead of a dollar. The formula resulting in 15 percent increases became known as the "Little Steel" formula.

Labor unions supported the "Little Steel" formula for they recognized that it was the only means of keeping prices in check and preventing inflation. By early 1943, when the cost of living had advanced dangerously, the government held the 15 percent pay rise formula and rolled back prices, a procedure which was successful in stemming inflation during the rest of the war.

"LITTLE STEEL" STRIKE

In 1937 the United States Steel Corporation, which had always been fiercely antilabor, negotiated an agreement with the Steel Workers Organizing Committee (SWOC). Without pressure from a strike, the company agreed to a ten percent wage increase, an eight-hour day, and a forty-hour week. Everywhere labor leaders and corporate officials were stunned by the news. In no time a hundred smaller steel companies signed up with the SWOC, leaving as the only holdouts Bethlehem Steel Corp., Inland Steel Co., Republic Steel Corp., and Youngstown Sheet and Tube Co., known as the "Little Steel" companies.

Tom Girdler, the antiunion president of Republic, was their leader. Although 75,000 men walked off their jobs, he refused to bargain with the union. Instead, back-to-work movements were begun, picket lines were smashed, union headquarters gassed, strike leaders arrested, and strikebreakers imported and protected by state militia.

Violence broke out in many towns; four men were killed and many injured. The climax came May 30 at the Republic Steel Company's plant in South Chicago when

150 policemen lined up to stop some 1,500 strikers who decided to march on the plant. After the crowd was ordered to disperse, the strikers threw a barrage of bricks, rocks, bolts, and other missiles at the police. Seconds later the unarmed strikers were running in every direction to escape the bullets and tear gas; ten were killed and eighty injured before order was restored.

Union labor leaders referred to the event as the "Memorial Day Massacre." A mass funeral was held for the dead and public sympathy was aroused, but nothing broke the stalemate. The Little Steel companies refused to sign up with the SWOC and eventually the men straggled back to work. Four years later each of the companies was ordered by the National Labor Relations Board to recognize the United Steelworkers of America (the new name for the SWOC), to rehire all employees who lost jobs because they had participated in strikes or joined a union, and to accept collective bargaining with the union. By 1941 this CIO affiliate had signed up 600,000 steel workers and union contracts had been negotiated in most of the industry.

LOCKOUT

When an employer closes up his company or shop in order to keep employees from working during a strike or labor dispute, it is called a lockout.

LOWELL GIRLS

During the 1820's a number of textile mills were built in Lowell, Massachusetts, along the river's edge because of the abundance of water power. Numerous young women were recruited from New England farms to tend the machines and became known as the "Lowell Girls."

The mill managements felt responsible for taking care

125

of these female operatives and acted not only as employers but as guardians and chaperones. Each employee agreed to obey company rules, be in her house by a certain hour and conduct herself like a lady. At night the young women were urged to improve their minds by listening to lectures, attending school, or reading. Many were so anxious to better themselves that after working thirteen hours, they would dress up and sit through a two or three hour lecture or class session.

When these employees returned home for a visit or to marry, they told friends how they, too, might make money in the Lowell mills. Parents had no qualms about letting their daughters work in these factories. After working a year or two, an operative who made a dollar and a half a week after paying for her board could save enough money for her dowry or tuition to prepare for teaching.

Working conditions deteriorated and in 1834 the Lowell girls struck for higher wages. The ringleaders were fired and blacklisted and subsequent work stoppages were seldom successful. In 1842 newer and faster machines were introduced and any girl who could not keep up with her quota was fired. At the same time wages were often paid in store orders rather than cash, and as textile competition grew, and profits diminished, the welfare of female employees was ignored. With the immigration of thousands of young girls from Ireland in 1848 following the severe potato famine, the mills were operated at starvation wages. The relatively good living conditions which the Lowell girls had once enjoyed were now forgotten.

LUDLOW MASSACRE

During the winter of 1903–1904, a strike called by the United Mine Workers (UMW) against the Colorado Fuel and Iron Company ended in a defeat for the union and deportation of many strikers. Ten years later, in September 1913, the UMW tried again to organize workers in the southern Colorado coal companies. When the managements refused to negotiate with the union, there was a strike call with demands for union recognition and wage increases before the men would return to work.

Some guards hired by the companies attacked a tent colony in Forbes where strikers were living. Others broke up a mass meeting held by the UMW. The governor imposed martial law whereupon pickets were scattered, strikers arrested, and leaders deported from the state. In April, 1914 a group of militia marched against the strikers' tents, this time in Ludlow. The troops killed two men and a boy before they burned the camp. Next day someone discovered that two women and eleven children who had fled from the soldiers had been smothered to death in a cave.

Branding the calamity "The Ludlow Massacre," the miners vowed revenge. After they had obtained weapons the men demolished mine properties, then they attacked both the state militia and company guards. Battles raged for a week until the governor asked for federal troops which promptly restored peace in the coal fields. The strike continued, but all attempts at settling it failed in spite of intervention by President Woodrow Wilson. The companies refused to capitulate and in December, 1914, the UMW called off the strike.

M

MEANY, GEORGE

George Meany, first president of the AFL-CIO, was born in New York City on August 16, 1894. At sixteen the young boy apprenticed in his father's trade as a plumber, joined the plumber's union, of which his father was president, and later, in 1922, became its business agent. His knowledge of unions and workingmen's problems helped him win the presidency of the New York State Federation of Labor in 1934 and in 1940 he swung over to the American Federation of Labor (AFL) as its secretary-treasurer.

During World War II he served on the War Labor Board and the National Defense Mediation Board. Following the war, he actively opposed the AFL's entry into the Russian dominated World Federation of Trade Unions because labor organizations in Soviet Russia were not "free or democratic." * Instead, he promoted membership in the International Confederation of Free Trade Unions (ICFTU), which the AFL had helped found in 1949.

In 1952, when William Green died, Meany was elected president of the AFL and immediately concentrated his attention on reunifying the AFL and the Congress of Industrial Organizations (CIO) which had been split for fifteen years. At the same time he worked out a "no-raiding" agreement with the CIO and was instrumental in expelling the corrupt International Longshoremen's Association from the AFL.

* The CIO affiliated in 1945 but withdrew in 1949.

On February 9, 1955, Meany signed a merger agreement on behalf of the AFL with Walter Reuther, president of the CIO, and the two men were thereupon elected president and vice president, respectively, of the new organization. After the merger, one of the first problems to command Meany's attention was the extensive corruption in certain labor unions which was revealed by the McClellan Committee hearings. In 1957 he expelled three member unions, including the Teamsters. That same year Meany was elected vice-president of the ICFTU and then served as a delegate to the United Nations General Assembly during 1957–58 and 1959–60.

Throughout his career Meany was outspoken against Communism, jurisdictional disputes, and corruption in unions. As he led the AFL-CIO into the decade of the 1970's, age did not appear to have dimmed his enthusiasm for serving the union cause.

(See also: American Federation of Labor; Congress of Industrial Organizations.)

MEDIATION

In mediation, a third party, or the mediator, recommends to the disagreeing parties various proposals or methods for settling their dispute. He does not impose any solution of his own but tries to lead the parties to work out their own answers. In conciliation, the conciliator merely brings the parties together and urges them to agree to any solutions which are freely offered by both sides.

The Taft-Hartley Act provided for establishment of the Federal Mediation and Conciliation Service. The Service has no law enforcement authority, but its mediators, who are located in seven regional offices and many industrial cities, rely wholly on persuasive techniques of mediation and conciliation to perform their duties.

The Service offers its facilities in labor-management disputes in any industry affecting interstate commerce, either on its own motion or at the request of one or more parties to the dispute. If the mediator cannot bring the representatives of management and labor to agreement, he tries to induce them to seek other means of settling the dispute, without resorting to a strike, lockout, or other form of coercion.

(See also: Arbitration; Conciliation.)

MIGRANT LABOR

Migrant laborers travel from place to place harvesting crops that must be picked as soon as they ripen. Investigations have revealed that many of these workers and their families have been forced to live in shockingly substandard conditions. They have been exploited and usually have had to work for very low wages.

During the early 1930's, a combination of the depression and devastating dust storms which ripped the topsoil from much of the land in Arkansas, Kansas, Oklahoma, and Texas caused a migration to the West Coast. It was estimated that 150,000 farmers and their families sought work in the California fruit orchards and vegetable farms as well as in lumber camps further north in Oregon and Washington. Known as "Okies" * they were often treated with brutality, deprived of their civil rights, and paid starvation wages.

On July 29, 1970, following almost five years of intermittent strikes and a national boycott, twenty-six major

* These migrants were called "Okies" because so many of them came from Oklahoma. John Steinbeck wrote about them in his novel *The Grapes of Wrath.*

grape growers in Delano, California signed contracts with the AFL-CIO's United Farm Workers Organizing Committee (UFWOC) headed by Cesar Chavez. This agreement brought an estimated 75 percent of the state's grape producers under the UFWOC and it was expected that the remaining growers would sign up shortly.

Meanwhile the Teamsters' Union had been organizing field hands and had signed up most of the vegetable crop growers in the Santa Maria area. Under a "peace pact" announced August 2, 1970, the Teamsters agreed to limit their activities to organizing cannery workers and let the UFWOC concentrate on organizing field workers.

A year later the country's first company-owned non-profit farm labor hiring hall was agreed to by Heublein Inc. and the UFWOC. This development, plus news that early in 1972 Cesar Chavez had negotiated an agreement with a major food grower on behalf of Florida agricultural workers, indicated that sometime soon most migratory workers could look forward to increased wages and better living conditions as they move from job to job picking the nation's food crops.

MITCHELL, JOHN

An early president of the United Mine Workers (UMW), John Mitchell was born in the mining town of Braidwood, Illinois, on February 4, 1870. There was little time for him to attend school because he had to help at home and when twelve he became a fulltime miner. He joined the Knights of Labor, then went west to work in various mines and returned to a Braidwood mine in 1888.

There Mitchell found that wages had been cut 20 percent because immigrants had crowded into the coal fields and agreed to work at reduced rates of pay. As the young man dug underground, he kept thinking about the miners' problems and how he might help to correct them. He accepted the post of secretary-treasurer of the UMW's northern Illinois subdistrict, and in 1897 was appointed union legislative representative at Springfield, the state capital.

In July of that same year, a national coal strike was called, but inasmuch as miners in the southern Illinois fields were unorganized, they did not join the work stoppage. Mitchell was sent there to sign up the men and did such a quick and thorough job that his accomplishments were noticed by the national UMW officers. The following January the UMW convention elected Mitchell vice-president and shortly thereafter, at the age of twenty-eight, president.

One of the first things Mitchell did was to visit the mines in eastern Pennsylvania. Here miners, mostly of foreign extraction, were reduced almost to a condition of servitude. They lived in squalor, were overworked, underpaid, cheated when their coal was weighed, and victimized by the company stores. Divided by race, language, religion, and suspicion, these men had been neglected and despised by native-born Americans because of their crude manners and lower standards of living. Union organizers had thought it hopeless to organize them.

Mitchell enlisted the help of local priests, pastors, and sympathetic civic leaders, preached the importance of unions, and reminded the public that these men had not had a wage increase for twenty years. After months of travel, meetings, conferences, speeches, and visits, he felt confident that the men would rally behind him.

A conference with the mine owners, backed by a strike in which all but ten thousand of the 140,000 miners participated, won some increases. When the contract expired in 1902, Mitchell called the men out on strike again. After six months of idleness, a truce was reached so that the men could return to work. An Anthracite Coal Strike Commission was appointed and the following March the men received a 10 percent increase, a nine-hour day, the use of arbitration and conciliation boards, but there was no recognition for the UMW. Although the men hailed Mitchell as their champion, he accepted the terms with great reluctance.

Plagued by poor health, he turned the presidency over to Tom L. Lewis (no relation to John L. Lewis, later president of the UMW), in 1907. During his ten year tenure, the union membership had grown from 33,000 to 260,000, and Mitchell had won decent wage scales and better working conditions for both anthracite and bituminous miners.

From 1915 until his death in New York City on September 9, 1919, Mitchell served as chairman of the New York State Industrial Commission. He was the author of two published books: *Organized Labor* (1903) and *The Wage Earner and His Problems* (1913). The epitaph on his tombstone reads: "Champion of Liberty—Defender of Human Rights."

(See also: Coal Strikes.)

MOLLY MAGUIRES

Founded as the Ancient Order of Hibernians in Ireland in 1843 to frighten process-servers sent by the English landlords, members of this secret society dressed in a type of women's clothing known as "Molly Maguires." They established a branch of the labor organization in Pennsylvania which was incorporated in 1871 as a "humane, charitable, and benevolent organization." The group then spread throughout the anthracite fields in that state and into West Virginia during the early 1870's.

The society aided its members in labor disputes by

adopting terror tactics which included arson and destruction of mine property and physical attacks on company personnel. After a Pinkerton detective, James McParlan, infiltrated the secret organization, twenty-four members were brought to trial in 1875. All were convicted, ten were executed, and the Mollies then disappeared.

(See also: Pinkerton Agency.)

MUCKRAKERS

President Theodore Roosevelt applied the term to a group of newspapermen and writers who called attention in articles and books to economic, social, and political evils, with the hope of bringing about corrective legislation or other action. These writers were part of the so-called progressive or reform movement which spanned the period from the 1890's until before World War I.

Upton Sinclair's novel *The Jungle* exposed the shocking conditions in the Chicago stockyards and led to passage, in 1906, of the Pure Food and Drug Act and the Meat Inspection Act. Other prominent writers included Ida Tarbell, Ray Stannard Baker, Frank Norris, and Henry Demarest Lloyd. Lloyd concentrated on calling attention to abuses suffered by labor, especially in factories and mines, and he pushed for compulsory arbitration of labor disputes. Illinois Governor John Peter Altgeld was one of the leading reform governors who worked for pioneer labor legislation as well as antitrust, civil service, tax, penal, and mental health reforms.

MURRAY, PHILIP

The son of an Irish coal miner, Philip Murray was born in Blantyre, Scotland, May 25, 1886. His mother died when he was two, making it necessary for the young child to stay close to his father as he worked. As a result, by the time he was ten Philip was a full-fledged miner. In 1902 father and son emigrated to the United States and worked in mines near Pittsburgh. During his limited spare time, Philip took correspondence courses in economics and mathematics and participated in athletic contests.

When eighteen, Murray had a fistfight with a weighman who tried to cheat him. The young miner was fired and his six hundred fellow miners went on strike. During their month-long strike, they elected Murray president of their local union of the United Mine Workers (UMW), but when the men returned to their jobs, Murray was forced to leave the company town. He then decided to dedicate himself to the union cause.

After he found another job, he became active in the affairs of the UMW and by 1920 had advanced to vice-presidency—the same year John L. Lewis was elected president. Although Murray was a Democrat and Lewis a Republican, the two worked well together, Murray becoming one of the chief negotiators. His courtesy, good humor, knowledge of the coal industry and ability with figures won him wide respect.

When Lewis organized the Committee for Industrial Organizations in 1935, Murray played an important part and the next year was Lewis' choice for chairman of the Steel Workers Organizing Campaign (SWOC) which signed up 125,000 members within six months. Speaking about Murray's tactics, *Barron's Weekly* stated: "For the first time in the history of the United States, industrial management is faced with a labor movement which is smart and courageous, wealthy and successful—a movement, moreover, which is winning its battle by applying a shrewd imitation of big business organization and technique."

In 1940 when Lewis retired from the Congress of Industrial Organizations (which he had organized in 1937 as a successor to the Committee for Industrial Organization), Murray was elected president. Two years later, the United Steelworkers of America (a new name for the SWOC) was organized and Murray was also elected president of that organization.

Murray and Lewis disagreed over a number of issues, and Murray accused Lewis in May, 1942, of being a man "hellbent on creating national confusion and national disunity." After forcing Murray to resign from the UMW, Lewis then took the UMW out of the CIO.

Following the end of World War II, Murray approached President William Green of the American Federation of Labor (AFL) to see if they could work out a merger as "protection against the ferocious attacks . . . being made upon labor." Misunderstandings between the two and other impediments prevented them from achieving unity. However, the death of both men in 1952 helped pave the way for the 1955 merger of the AFL-CIO.

Philip Murray died in San Francisco, California on November 9, 1952. A labor leader of stature, integrity, and eloquence, he has been considered by some as the equal of Samuel Gompers, founder of the AFL.

N ••

NATIONAL COLORED LABOR UNION

In December, 1869, a number of Negro intellectuals and trade unionists met and founded the National Colored Labor Union (NCLU). Their platform, naturally, emphasized the problem of discrimination which was called "an insult to God, an injury to us, and a disgrace to humanity." The platform also called for cooperative Negro workshops to provide employment for the members who were excluded "from other workshops on account of color."

During the following year, Isaac Myers conducted an organizing drive throughout the southern states, hoping to forestall the time when Negroes, now emancipated, would be excluded from skilled trades. He also wanted to show white unionists that Negroes were responsible citizens and could be relied upon to take their place in the trade-unionism movement.

The leadership tried to affiliate the union with the National Labor Union, but the fifth congress of that organization declared itself in favor of having the NCLU remain outside as an independent labor party. This exclusion was fatal to the NCLU since it made it a separate and segregated organization which would have had little if any influence in representing its membership.

NATIONAL INDUSTRIAL RECOVERY ACT

In order to spur industrial recovery during the Depression of the 1930's, this act, popularly known as the NIRA

137

National Industrial Recovery Act

or NRA, was signed into law by President Franklin D. Roosevelt on June 16,1933.

The statute provided for "self-regulation" of business through industry codes to eliminate overproduction and cutthroat competition. Prices could be increased to produce a reasonable profit, and labor was protected by guarantees of a minimum wage, reasonable hours of work, and the right of collective bargaining. Under the law each division of commerce and industry established a committee representing labor, management, and the public, to draw up and adopt a code which would be observed by all who signed it.* Each employer who signed was given a Blue Eagle emblem to display in his place of business. To get the program under way, $3,300,000,000 was appropriated for a public works program to stimulate the economy and put men to work again.

The most famous part of the NIRA was Section 7(a) which stipulated that every code should contain these three guarantees: (1) that employees could organize and bargain collectively; (2) that no employee could be prevented from joining a labor union or forced to join a company union; and (3) that employers must pay minimum wage rates and observe maximum hours of work and other employment rules set forth in the code adopted by the industry. To administer this section Congress established the National Labor Board in 1933. A year later it was replaced, on July 9, 1934, by the National Labor Relations Board. This board operated independently of the National Recovery Administration headed by General Hugh S. Johnson who administered all of the other provisions of the NIRA.

* The act provided that antitrust laws were suspended temporarily so that businesses could collaborate and work together to fix prices without being prosecuted.

On "Black Monday", May 25, 1935, in the case of *Schechter Poultry Corporation v. United States,* the Supreme Court declared the NIRA unconstitutional because Congress had extended its authority beyond interstate commerce to intrastate commerce and had also delegated authority without spelling out how it should be exercised.

The NIRA was superseded by the National Labor Relations Act which did not include the Blue Eagle industry codes but concentrated on giving labor the protections it had sought for such a long time.

(See also: Depression of the 1930's; National Labor Relations Board; New Deal.)

NATIONAL LABOR RELATIONS ACT

Known also as the Wagner Act, the National Labor Relations Act (NLRA) has often been called the cornerstone of President Franklin D. Roosevelt's New Deal program for labor. When it became apparent that the National Industrial Recovery Act was a failure, Senator Robert Wagner introduced his bill which retained and tightened the controversial Section 7(a).*

The new law, signed by the President of July 5, 1935, established a three man National Labor Relations Board (later increased to five members by the Taft-Hartley Act) to administer its provisions in accordance with the principle that employees have the "right to self-organization, to form, join or assist labor organizations to bargain collectively through representatives of their own choosing, and to engage in concerted activities for the purpose of collective bargaining or other mutual aid or protection."

---

* Section 7(a) provided that every NRA code and agreement should guarantee the right of employees to organize and bargain collectively through their representatives without interference, restraint, or coercion by employers.

The NLRA guaranteed workers the right to organize, join labor unions, and bargain collectively with employers. It also defined unfair labor practices committed by employers and which were thereafter declared illegal.

Two weeks after the act was adopted the American Liberty League issued a statement signed by fifty-eight lawyers who asserted that the law was unconstitutional. Earl F. Reed, counsel to the Weirton Steel Company and chairman of the Liberty League committee, said he would advise his clients not to feel bound by a law which he considered unconstitutional.

In a short time the Supreme Court was forced to consider a number of cases designed to test the constitutionality of the NLRA. In *National Labor Relations Board v. Jones and Laughlin Steel Company,* the court upheld the constitutionality of the law, and during the years that followed the court also supported the numerous rulings which the National Labor Relations Board handed down to enforce the law.

(See also: National Industrial Recovery Act; National Labor Relations Board; New Deal.)

NATIONAL LABOR RELATIONS BOARD

An independent federal agency created by the National Labor Relations Act, the National Labor Relations Board (NLRB) has five members,* each of whom is appointed by the President, with approval of the Senate, for a five-year term.

The Board has two principal functions: (1) remedying and preventing unfair labor practices by employers and labor organizations or their agents, and (2) conducting,

* The National Labor Relations Act originally provided for three members but the Board was increased to five in 1947 by the Taft-Hartley Act.

for the purpose of collective bargaining, secret ballot elections among employees to determine whether or not they want to be represented by a labor organization. The Board also holds secret ballot elections among employees who are covered by a union agreement to determine whether or not they want to revoke their agreements with the union. In jurisdictional disputes, the Board decides which competing group of workers is entitled to perform the work involved, and in national emergency labor disputes, the Board arranges for secret ballot elections among employees who wish to vote on the employers' final settlement offers.

In addition to the above activities, the Board is authorized to prohibit "unfair" employer practices such as refusing to bargain collectively with representatives of its employees, supporting company unions, interfering with employees who want to exercise their rights guaranteed by law, hiring or firing to encourage membership in a company union, or discriminating against an employee because he complained to the NLRB.

The Board has the right to make rules and regulations, hold hearings, subpoena witnesses, and issue final orders. It enforces its decisions by promulgating "cease and desist" orders and when necessary by obtaining enforcement orders from the United States Court of Appeals.

(See also: National Labor Relations Act; New Deal.)

NATIONAL LABOR UNION

In August, 1866, seventy-seven trade union delegates representing sixty thousand workers in thirteen states met in Baltimore to create the "first National Labor Congress ever convened in the United States." The purpose of the convention was to unify the ranks of labor. The organizers of the new union planned to extend membership not only

141

to skilled workers who were already unionized, but also to unorganized workers who would include unskilled laborers and farmers.

From the beginning the party's membership was divided into two factions. One reflected the idealism of the 1830's and 1840's when workingmen's parties were politically conscious and determined to win humanitarian reforms. The other group endorsed the trade unionist philosophy which had developed just before the Civil War. These members dominated the union as they worked to increase the membership, win an eight-hour day, and eliminate the competition of cheap labor.

When representatives of women's and Negro groups approached the National Labor Union (NLU), their delegates were admitted to the union's congresses. However, members were suspicious of women's labor organizations and never actively supported them. In the case of Negro members, most NLU delegates viewed them as cheap labor competition, and when the National Colored Labor Union was formed refused to give it affiliation.

In 1868 William H. Sylvis (1828–1869), a journeyman molder who had learned his trade as an apprentice near his birthplace, Annoph, Pennsylvania, was elected president of the NLU. Sylvis worked hard to build up the union, advocated collective bargaining, and backed strikes only if they were used as a last resort to gain the workers' goals. During his brief leadership Sylvis concentrated on promoting labor reforms through political action and his death in 1869 was a serious blow, not only to the union but to trade in unionism in general.

Early in 1872 a hundred union delegates from fourteen states held a convention in Columbus, Ohio, to consider what political action the NLU should take in the forthcoming presidential election. They chose the name of

142

Labor Reform Party for this political arm of the union. Then they adopted a party platform and nominated David Davis of Illinois, associate justice of the Supreme Court, and John Parker, governor of New Jersey, as their presidential and vice presidential candidates. The nominations split both the convention and the union itself. Some workingmen's committees demanded new nominations, whereupon Davis withdrew and the executive committee of the Labor Reform Party nominated Charles O'Connor of Tammany Hall as their presidential candidate. He polled less than thirty thousand votes, and when the seventh general convention was held late that year, seven delegates attended. The disappointed attendees admitted that the party was dead in spite of its membership of 600,000 and returned sadly to their homes.

(See also: National Colored Labor Union.)

NEW DEAL

When Franklin D. Roosevelt accepted the Democratic Party nomination for President in 1932, he referred to his proposed program of reform legislation as the New Deal. The New Deal was based on Roosevelt's belief that government should assume more responsibility for the welfare of all Americans. After President Roosevelt's inauguration, Congress enacted numerous laws which brought about sweeping changes in three broad areas: immediate relief for people who were in need; economic assistance for agriculture and business; and economic and social reforms. The major programs included public works to stimulate business and industry, economic relief for farmers, public housing for low-income workers, new laws to guarantee labor the right to organize unions and engage in collective bargaining, social security for the aged, regulation of banking and finance to strengthen banks and securities exchanges, jobs for unemployed youth and cheaper public power for rural areas.

One of the New Deal's unusual economic solutions was adoption of the National Industrial Recovery Act of 1933 which established NRA industry codes to regulate every branch of business. The government and business leaders who administered each of the codes were authorized to set minimum prices, wages and quality standards. Most businessmen accepted the codes at first, but later objected to these restraints and the stifling of competition. In 1935 the Supreme Court declared the NRA unconstitutional.

The speed of reform slowed up after 1937, and the New Deal leaders gradually shifted much of their attention to foreign affairs as war broke out in Europe and then involved the United States. In spite of the sudden switch in the United States to a total war economy, most of the New Deal reform legislation survived World War II.

(See also: Depression of 1930's.)

O

OPEN SHOP

In an open shop a company may employ either union or non-union workers. In practice this enables an employer to discriminate against a union because in an open shop there generally is no group of employees who can force an employer to engage in collective bargaining.

(See also: American Plan; Closed Shop.)

P ··

PATERSON SILK STRIKE

In 1913 organizers of the Industrial Workers of the World (IWW) invaded Paterson, New Jersey, to help the silk workers who were on strike. The union had won a significant victory the previous year for textile workers in Lawrence, Massachusetts, and its executive committee felt that they could do as much for the strikers in Paterson. Joseph J. Ettor and William ("Big Bill) Haywood, two of the IWW leaders, arrived in New Jersey and went to work signing up the men on strike.

The Paterson police, aware of the trouble which the union caused in Lawrence, had no intention of letting the IWW take over and triumph in their town. For five months the police and workers fought, picket lines were broken up, strikers were clubbed, often into insensibility, and numerous arrests were made on trumped up charges. Finally, when union funds had been depleted and families of strikers became destitute, the men were forced to return to their jobs without winning a single concession from their employers.

This strike was important because it marked a turning point in the history of the IWW. Thereafter the union suffered a succession of defeats wherever it attempted to represent workingmen who were striking for better wages or working conditions. Within five years the union practically disappeared from the labor scene.

(See also: William Haywood; Industrial Workers of the World; Lawrence Textile Strike.)

145

PENSIONS

A pension or retirement benefit system provides monthly or annual payments for employees of a business or government when they retire. The amount an individual receives is related to his length of service and the financial contributions which he and/or his employer have made into the pension fund. Survivors of a retired employee may also continue to receive his pension in the same or a reduced amount. Originally pensions were personal gifts from a king or other sovereign to soldiers for distinguished military service. Later, pensions were also granted to those who made significant contributions to the arts, literature, and science.

By the 1850's the factory system had developed to the point where large numbers of employees were working at low-paying jobs and were unable to earn or save enough for their old age. Furthermore, many older men and women lost their jobs to younger people and could not find other employment. As a result there was widespread agitation for government or industry to provide old age assistance, this being especially true in Europe. As early as 1833 Great Britain had instituted a plan for making retirement benefits available to those who subscribed to a special program. In 1850 Belgium and France both sponsored savings funds for old age pensions. Four years later Prussia established pension funds supported by compulsory payments for firemen, miners, policemen, railroad workers, and other groups. In the United States, the modern pension systems operated by business and government scarcely appeared until after 1935 when the New Deal instituted the Social Security system. This socialized insurance encouraged development of private retirement plans for workers in business and industry.

In the private sector most businesses of any size offer employees a retirement plan. Group plans are available for clergy, physicians, college professors, and other professional workers. In addition, it is possible for an individual to purchase life insurance or annuities and arrange the policies in such a way that he will receive monthly payments for life starting at age sixty-five or whenever he elects.

There are many government systems, the most important of which include: Old Age Assistance (Social Security), military pensions, widows' pensions, the Railroad Retirement System, teacher retirement systems, and federal, state, county, and municipal government retirement systems.

The mechanics and mathematics of establishing a pension system are extremely complex, and every retirement plan must be based on a sound actuarial or statistical basis. This takes into account the expected life span of the beneficiaries and the anticipated death rate of the insured before retirement. It also means that premiums must be sufficiently large to cover the costs and that ample reserves are set aside to make certain there will always be enough cash on hand to make the monthly payments.

In contributory pensions, both employees and employers make payments to the plan. In a non-contributory pension plan, the employer pays all of the premiums. In profit sharing plans, the amount of the retirement benefits are based on how much profit was available to purchase retirement insurance. If a plan provides "vested rights," an employee will receive his pension at the normal retirement age on the basis of what he and the company have contributed, even though he has been fired or resigned before reaching normal retirement age. Usually a pension is not vested until the employee has worked and been contributing for at least ten or fifteen years.

(See also: Railroad Retirement Acts; Social Security.)

PEONAGE

Peonage was a system of forced labor which required a *peon* (Spanish for laborer) to work in order to pay up his debts. This was a common custom in the Spanish colonies until the early 1900's when the system was abolished in most countries.

The practice also existed in the United States. It was notorious in Arizona and New Mexico following the Civil War when in some towns the authorities would arrest Negroes on false charges and impose large fines. Those who could not pay were forced to work for a certain time without wages for whomever paid the fine. When the period of forced labor was completed, the victims were released and then often rearrested and compelled to repeat the cycle.

In 1911 all kinds of peonage were declared unconstitutional by the U.S. Supreme Court.

PERKINS, FRANCES

Frances Perkins the first woman to serve in the United States Cabinet, was born on April 10, 1882, in Boston, Massachusetts. She grew up in nearby Worcester, went to Mount Holyoke College where she majored in biology and chemistry, and after graduation returned home to do social work for two years. Next she took a position teaching chemistry in a Chicago girls' school and decided to live at Hull House.* After school she spent her spare time visiting sweatshops and tenements with friends who were

* A famous settlement house founded in 1889 by Jane Addams and Ellen Gates Starr.

social workers. This experience convinced her that she should enter the social work profession. Once she had received a Master's degree from Columbia University in 1910, she became executive secretary of the New York Consumers' League which was concerned with improving industrial conditions and supporting protective laws for women and children.

In 1911 Miss Perkins watched the Triangle Shirtwaist Factory fire and was so shocked by the tragedy that she spent the next six years working on laws to promote industrial safety. She was also responsible for regulations imposed on the numerous cellar bakeries that dotted New York City at that time and became executive secretary of the New York Committee on Safety. Another of her concerns was to back legislation setting a maximum fifty-four-hour workweek for women workers, an activity which gave her opportunity to meet the state political leaders including Robert F. Wagner and Franklin D. Roosevelt.

Miss Perkins married Paul Caldwell Wilson, a financial statistician, in 1913 and had one daughter, managing at the same time to keep active on various committees. Appointed to the New York State Industrial Commission, she worked for labor and industrial legislation, succeeded in having the fifty-four-hour week for women reduced to forty-eight, and was responsible for other reforms. When Franklin D. Roosevelt became Governor of New York, he appointed Miss Perkins his Industrial Commissioner, and after he entered the White House, he named her his Secretary of Labor, a post she held from 1933–1945.

Organized labor opposed the appointment, criticized her "welfare outlook," complained because she could not bring about peace between the AFL and CIO, and pointed out that she was ineffective in helping settle major strikes. A House Resolution was introduced asking the Judiciary Committee to decide whether or not she should be impeached for failing to deport Harry Bridges. The resolution was defeated but hearings were held on deportation charges.

Nevertheless, even her critics respected Miss Perkins' integrity and the way she always stuck by her principles. Much of the social reform legislation of the New Deal was said to have been due largely to her influence. One of her significant contributions was achieved while she served as chairman of the President's Committee on Economic Security and helped prepare the committee's report which provided the framework for the Social Security Act.

Miss Perkins resigned her post two months after President Roosevelt's death, and the following year President Harry Truman appointed her to the United States Civil Service Commission where she served until 1952. Thereafter she spent much of her time traveling and giving lectures on labor relations. She died in New York City on May 14, 1965.

(See also: New Deal; Franklin D. Roosevelt; Triangle Shirtwaist Factory Fire.)

PETRILLO, JAMES CAESAR

A tough labor boss, often called the "Mussolini of music," James C. Petrillo was born in Chicago on March 16, 1892. He began to play the trumpet when he was eight and became a member of the *Daily News* band. After nine years of school he finally completed the fourth grade, and at fourteen he quit and organized his own orchestra. Here he played the trumpet "loud but lousy" (his own words), until he switched to the drums. At one time he also ran a cigar stand, then had part ownership in a saloon, and finally entered union politics, becoming president of the local independent American Musicians' Union at twenty-two. He kept this job for three years until he lost an election, whereupon he quit the union, joined the American Federation of Musicians (AFM) and by 1922 was its president.

A born fighter, he first tackled the radio stations when broadcasting started to affect musicians' jobs. He won a five-day week for seven days' pay, forced the stations to join the local union or pay musicians to stand by and do nothing, and stipulated that those operating the record players had to be union musicians paid union rates.

In 1927, when the Chicago theaters opposed him, two thousand musicians struck, but four days later returned to work because the theaters were now members of Petrillo's union. In 1931 Chicago hotels were forced to sign with the union under threat of no music for New Year's Eve. Petrillo forbade musicians in Chicago to make recordings for use by broadcasting stations; he negotiated a contract which gave the AFM control over canned music from most radio stations; high school bands could not be used to provide music for organizations if a union band were available; the Boston Symphony, at one time the only non-union group, was prevented from making recordings. The list of orders and prohibitions issued by this labor czar are seemingly endless.

By using strike pressures, Petrillo was able to fight the technological threats that faced musicians as activities of film industries and record companies eliminated many of their jobs. Probably his greatest triumph was achieved in 1942 when recording companies agreed to pay a royalty to the musicians' union for every record sold.

After resigning as president of the AFM, Petrillo continued as president of the Chicago branch of the same union until his resignation in 1963.

PINKERTON AGENCY

The Pinkerton Agency (now Pinkerton's Inc.) was established in 1850 by Allan Pinkerton who was born in Glasgow, Scotland, in 1819 and emigrated to Chicago in 1842. He set up a cooper's shop and held various county sheriff jobs until 1850 when he became the only detective on the Chicago police force and also opened the Pinkerton Agency. Pinkerton's sympathies lay with the moneyed industrialists, and his firm was, therefore, destined to become one of organized labor's foremost enemies for the next hundred years.

At first Pinkerton specialized in railroad theft cases. In 1855 he contracted with the Illinois Central Railroad and several other lines to provide police protection. In 1861 he uncovered a plot to assassinate President-elect Lincoln. With Kate Warne, a female operative, he "spirited" Lincoln safely through Baltimore to Washington and later that year was appointed head of the United States Secret Service. While serving in this post he operated his Chicago office and established branches in other cities.

In 1877 the agency made newspaper headlines after its agent, James McParlan, helped break up the Molly Maguires, a secret terrorist society. Thereafter Pinkerton's National Detective Agency became active in numerous strikebreaking activities, there being few major industrial conflicts in which its armed men, known as "Pinkerton Men," were not involved. The Homestead Strike of 1893 showed the Pinkertons in a familiar role.

Allan Pinkerton died in Chicago, July 1, 1884, and his son William Allan succeeded him. Although the company was hated by unions, its methods were always legal although sometimes of questionable morality. In an era when it was more popular to attack the workingman than

152

help him, Pinkerton's behavior was no worse than that of the industrialists who contracted for their services.

(See also: Homestead Strike; Molly Maguires.)

PORTAL-TO-PORTAL PAY

The period which covers the time an employee enters the company gate until he leaves the gate at the end of his workday is considered the basis for portal-to-portal pay. This concept originated in the coal mines where the union argued that it was unfair for a man to have to spend his time traveling from the entrance to the company's property to the actual mine portal.

It was held that under the Wage and Hour Law portal-to-portal pay was permitted and that an employer must pay an employee for all the time spent on his property, including both preparation for the job as well as any cleanup or other necessary activities after he had completed his work. On June 10, 1946, the Supreme Court ruled in the *Mount Clemens Pottery Company* case that under the Fair Labor Standards Act employers were liable for portal-to-portal pay.

As soon as the court decision was published, thousands of employee groups and unions filed claims with employers for back pay amounting to billions of dollars. Many companies faced bankruptcy and asked Congress to rescue them from certain ruin. The response was the Portal-to-Portal Act of 1947 which relieved employers of past liability for portal-to-portal pay. The law also provided that employers did not have to make such payments unless they were provided for in union contracts or by the tradition of the job or industry, thus depriving most unorganized employees of an opportunity to obtain portal-to-portal pay.

153

POWDERLY, TERENCE VINCENT

Terence V. Powderly, a famous labor leader, was born in Carbondale, Pennsylvania, on January 22, 1849. He became a railroad worker at age thirteen and served an apprenticeship in a machine shop. When he was twenty-two, he joined the Machinists' and Blacksmiths' Union and became its president the following year. In 1874 he was initiated into the Knights of Labor (which was still a secret society) and in 1879 achieved election to the highest office, Grand Master Workman.

Under Powderly's direction the Knights of Labor became the largest labor federation in the country. By 1886 there were more than 700,000 members but by 1893 a number of reverses had caused the membership to decline to less than 75,000. That same year Powderly resigned in a policy dispute with other union officials.

Powderly was an idealist and reformer who advocated abolishing the wage system in favor of cooperatively owned workshops. He once said that the "aim of the Knights of Labor—properly understood—is to make each man his own employer." Although his plan to accomplish this was quite vague, many people feared he was a radical. He favored industrial unions and was unenthusiastic over craft organizations because he felt that skilled workers should support the unskilled. This attitude caused many members to resign and ultimately to join the newly organized American Federation of Labor. Never a typical fighter or aggressive labor leader but one who prepared to conduct boycotts rather than strikes, Powderly would gladly have settled all labor disputes through arbitration.

The year after he resigned from the Knights of Labor, Powderly was admitted to the Pennsylvania bar. As a reward for having campaigned for President William McKinley, he was appointed U.S. Commissioner-General

of Immigration in 1897. From 1907–1921 he served as chief of the Division of Information of the Bureau of Immigration and then held various other government posts until his death in Washington, D.C. on June 24, 1924.
(See also: Knights of Labor.)

PRISONERS' UNIONS

Early in February, 1972, spokesmen for inmates of New York State's Green Haven prison notified State Correction Commissioner Russell G. Oswald that they had formed the "Prisoners Labor Union at Green Haven" and wanted it to be recognized as the exclusive bargaining agent for all the prisoners. At the same time the prisoners announced that District 65, Distributive Workers of America, had agreed to accept their union as an affiliate.

An attorney for the union stated that inasmuch as the inmates worked for the state they were entitled to collective bargaining rights under the state's Public Employers Fair Employment Act. Although prisoners do not have the right to quit their jobs, and the employer (in this case the prison) does not choose its work force, it appeared possible that there were some issues involving wages and working conditions which might be negotiated. It was conceivable that this might be a constructive step in bringing about some additional prison reform, which, according to most surveys, was greatly needed.

Although Commissioner Oswald quickly refused to recognize the prisoners' union, the organization had the backing of the Legal Aid Society and undoubtedly there would be many other supporters for the project. This was not the first prison union to be formed. Another had been organized in Los Angeles but it was not exclusively for inmates since it included families and certain individuals.

155

PROFESSIONAL WORKERS' UNIONS

For several decades certain workers have belonged to unions organized just for professionally trained men and women. Airline pilots, screen writers, teachers, movie photographers, writers, and newspaper reporters are included in this group. Recently unions have been organizing engineers and even some librarians have been joining unions.

The unionization of professional workers seems destined to grow as established industrial and craft unions expand. In 1970 the Teamsters' Union not only opened its ranks to teachers who did not want to join one of the three conventional teacher unions, but also to nurses, screen cartoonists, stockbrokers, and even attorneys. That same year *Newsday* editorial employees chose the United Auto Workers Union over the Newspaper Guild as their bargaining agent. Meanwhile the Amalgamated Meat Cutters Union was increasing its membership by signing up law enforcement officers. Apparently the large body of higher income professional workers as well as the many government employees was a tempting target for many unions seeking to broaden their memberships.

The Council of AFL-CIO Unions for Scientific, Professional and Cultural Employees (SPACE) was organized in Washington, D.C. in March, 1967. The goals of the council included mutual cooperation among members of scientific, professional, and cultural unions, encouragement of all professionals to become union members, participation in legislative activities that are of interest to professionals, and promotion of greater public interest in scientific, educational, and cultural activities. The council consisted of eighteen participating unions.

PROFIT SHARING

In a profit sharing plan each employee who participates receives his share of the net profits in accordance with a formula which is usually based on length of service and salary.

Many industrialists believe that a profit sharing plan makes employees feel that they have a stake in the business and that it encourages them to work harder and remain with the company. Others say that because workers do not share any of the risks of running a business they should not share in the profits.

Some labor leaders oppose profit sharing because they believe that workers are better off if they bargain for higher wages and that it is preferable for a man to receive a steady wage rather than have his income rise and fall with the company's profits. Other labor leaders are enthusiastic over the idea, however.

 ••

QUILL, MICHAEL JOSEPH

"Mike" Quill, as the founder of the Transport Workers Union of America (TWUA) was best known, was born September 18, 1905, in Gourtloughera, Ireland. He emigrated to the United States in 1926 and worked at various jobs before joining the New York City Interborough

Rapid Transit Company. Promotion to change maker in a booth earned him thirty-three cents an hour for a twelve-hour night shift, seven nights a week.

The IRT union agreed in 1932 to a 10 percent wage cut in order to help the company which was in receivership. Quill talked with friends about starting an independent union but nothing happened until April, 1934, when he and six fellow employees met to organize a union which they later named the Transport Workers Union of America (TWUA). The first "Transport Workers Bulletin" issued April 15, 1934 stated that the union's aim was to "safeguard, protect and improve the working conditions and living standards of all transport workers regardless of race, color, creed, nationality, or political views or affiliations." The union grew so rapidly that the following year it employed a full-time organizer, and in 1936 Quill resigned his IRT job to become its president.

In 1937 the new Congress of Industrial Organizations (CIO) granted the TWUA an international charter and Quill signed contracts with the three subway systems in New York City as well as the principal bus and trolley lines. That September Quill became the first International President of the TWUA and an executive board member of the CIO. The TWUA then proceeded to organize transportation and taxi workers in other cities. Subsequently it extended its organizing efforts into the air transportation industry in 1942 and the rail lines in 1954.

One of Quill's major goals was to win a forty-hour week for transit workers. This was achieved by strike threats, slowdowns, and strikes which greatly inconvenienced the public. Quill was often described as one of the most colorful modern labor leaders who thrived on controversy and achieved great advances for his membership.

On January 1, 1966, Quill called a twelve-day paralyzing transit strike in New York City in defiance of a court injunction. Two days later he and eight other union leaders were found guilty of contempt and sentenced to prison. Just two hours later Quill suffered a seizure, was rushed to the hospital, and died there on January 28th.

R •••

RAILROAD BROTHERHOODS

The four largest unions of railroad workers were the Brotherhood of Locomotive Engineers (founded in 1863), Conductors (1868), Firemen and Enginemen (1873), and Railway Trainmen (1883). They were organized as benefit societies to make life insurance available to their members but later became involved in labor activities. All of these brotherhoods, except the Brotherhood of Locomotive Engineers, have merged with other unions or changed their names and broadened their memberships.

RAILROAD LABOR ACTS

Railway Transportation Act of 1920. This law was also known as the Esch-Cummins Act. Essentially its purpose was to ease the return of the railroads, which were federally operated during World War I, to their owners. The statute also appropriated $200,000,000 to help railroads get back to a pre-war status, and a $300,000,000 revolving fund so loans might be made to financially weaker roads.

Railroad Labor Acts

A Railway Labor Board of nine members was created to settle labor disputes, but the board was powerless to enforce its decisions. Most of the other features of the law also proved ineffective either because railroad managements opposed them or the Supreme Court invalidated them.

Railway Labor Act of 1926. The Watson-Parker Act, or Railway Labor Act of 1926, abolished the old Railway Labor Board and provided for a National Mediation Board of five members which was empowered to mediate any dispute which had not been settled by direct negotiation or boards of adjustment. If the Board failed to settle a disagreement, it was instructed to try to induce the parties to submit the question to a court of arbitration whose decision would be binding. If this court failed, the President was authorized to appoint an emergency board to investigate and report to him. The railroads failed to cooperate in establishing the boards and the act proved ineffective.

Railway Labor Act of 1934. This, the third such act within fourteen years, also known as the Crosser-Dill Act, abolished the five member National Mediation Board and provided for a three man board. The principal duty of the smaller tribunal was to mediate differences between railroads, express, Pullman companies, and airlines on the one hand, and employees on the other. The Board was also authorized to hold elections to determine the proper representatives of employees. In addition to the top National Mediation Board, regional or railroad system boards were established.

The act provided for arbitration in certain situations. When arbitration failed, the Board could ask the President to appoint a fact-finding board for a thirty day period of investigation during which time the labor conditions would not be changed and there would be no strike. In addition to this machinery for settling disputes, the National Railway Adjustment Board was established to handle individual grievances involving interpretation of contracts.

The Railway Labor Act of 1934 also made it unlawful for carriers to interfere with any organizing of employees, to compel employees to join or not join a union, or to force employees to sign "yellow-dog" contracts.

RAILROAD RETIREMENT ACTS

A law passed in 1934 granted retirement payments to certain railroad employees but was declared unconstitutional by the Supreme Court the following March. In May, 1937, a new Railroad Retirement Act was passed and amended in 1951. The amendment increased the benefits and guaranteed that no beneficiary would receive less than those who are covered by the Social Security System.

A three man Railroad Retirement Board administers the Railroad Retirement and Railroad Unemployment Insurance Acts and the Health Insurance for the Aged Act insofar as it affects railroad retirement beneficiaries.

RAILROAD STRIKES

During the more than 140 years that trains have been running in the United States, there have been countless strikes.

Strike of 1877. On July 17, 1877, trainmen struck the Baltimore and Ohio Railroad in Martinsburg, West Virginia, and started the first major strike in American railroad history. A series of wage cuts, uncertain employment, blacklisting of union members, and other grievances had produced widespread distrust and resentment among the railroad workers. President Rutherford Hayes sent two

161

hundred federal soldiers to break the strike in Martinsburg, but meanwhile word of the work stoppage had spread, and strikes broke out in numerous other places and spread to other lines.

The worst trouble occurred in Pittsburgh where the local militia joined the strikers. Six hundred militiamen were then dispatched to Pittsburgh from Philadelphia, but they were attacked by a ferocious mob which drove them from the city. Meanwhile, under mob rule, some $5,000,000 worth of railroad property was destroyed.

By August 2 when railroad service had been restored throughout the nation, hundreds of people had been killed, unkown numbers injured, and some $10,000,000 worth of property damage was done. As a result many state legislatures enacted new conspiracy laws to curb labor unions, and armories were built in several cities to help strengthen the local militia.

Strikes of 1884 and 1885. Strikes were called on the Union Pacific Railroad during 1884 to protest wage cuts. This gave the Knights of Labor opportunity to step in and negotiate quick settlements in favor of the men. The following February and March, when workers struck three of Jay Gould's roads after he had cut wages by 10 percent, the Knights again intervened and the wage cut was rescinded. This success which the Knights had with Gould's railroads rocketed their membership from 104,000 in July 1885 to 703,000 a year later.

Strike of 1886. In March, 1886, a Knight was discharged from Gould's Southwestern Railway System and immediately some men walked out, charging discrimination. This time Gould's railroads fought the strikers by bringing in Pinkerton guards and strikebreakers and asking governors to call out the militia. The railroad managements refused to discuss the matter with representatives of the Knights, and a congressional investigation was instituted. Terence Powderly, Grand Master Workman of the Knights, saw no way to settle the strike and ordered the men to return to their jobs. The strike fizzled, and this proved one of several crushing defeats for the Knights which led to their early demise.

The Pullman Strike of 1894. In May, 1894, when an employee committee of the Pullman Company asked to discuss their grievances, they were refused. Shortly thereafter three members of the committee who belonged to the American Railway Union (ARU) were fired. All the employees struck; George R. Pullman locked the plant and said he would wait until the men were hungry enough to return to work. He was encouraged by the General Managers' Association, a group of railroad executives, who were anxious to use this strike as a means of destroying the ARU.

The union, then a year old, had been formed in June 1893 by Eugene V. Debs, who had tried to arbitrate with Mr. Pullman but was refused. Debs declared that if arbitration were not accepted by June 26, "the members of the American Railway Union shall refuse to handle Pullman cars and equipment on and after that date." The railroads then fired every man who joined the strike and soon 60,000 men were out and railroad operations were disrupted nationwide.

Trouble started in Chicago after mail cars were attached to a Pullman train thus making it an offense to halt the United States mail. A thousand deputy marshals were recruited to back up an order to disperse which was read to a crowd massed on the Rock Island Railroad's property at Blue Island (south of Chicago). The force was then increased by 2,600 deputies, many of whom the Chicago police called "thugs, thieves and ex-convicts."

Railroad Strikes

The strikers and the crowd then burned freight cars, signal towers, and freight awaiting shipment. Federal troops and state militia moved in and this only served to anger the crowds more. Debs asked trade unions in Chicago to start sympathy strikes but they refused. The ARU leaders realized they were powerless to win any concessions for the Pullman workers or promises from the railroads that they would take the strikers back without discrimination. The strikers suffered total defeat, the ARU was badly weakened, its leaders were imprisoned, and three years later the union was dissolved.

A circuit court ruled that the strike leaders had engaged in a conspiracy to restrain interstate commerce under the terms of the Sherman Antitrust Act.* The Supreme Court upheld the lower court, and this had the effect of declaring that the federal government had authority to intervene whenever anyone obstructed interstate commerce or transportation of the mails.

Strike of 1946. When wage negotiations between railroad workers and the carriers broke down, the Railway Labor Act failed to solve the impasse, and an emergency board succeeded in working out terms acceptable to all unions except the 300,000 Railroad Trainmen and Locomotive Engineers. May 18th was named as the strike deadline.

President Harry Truman ordered the railroads to be seized the day before the strike deadline and won a five day postponement of any stoppage, but on May 23 all trains stopped running. The President appealed to the

---

* This law, the first of several antitrust statutes designed to curb the growth of monopolies and monopoly practices, was adopted in 1890. It prohibited contracts or combinations which restrained foreign or interstate commerce or monopolized any part of interstate commerce.

strikers, declaring that this was a strike against the government. "The government must meet the challenge or confess its impotence." If the men did not return to work by four o'clock the next afternoon, he said, the government would operate the trains and the armed forces would provide protection. As the deadline approached, President Truman addressed a joint session of Congress to ask legal backing for his policy. He requested authority to deprive strikers of seniority rights, to draft them into the armed forces, and to obtain an injunction against the strike leaders. At this very moment a clerk handed him a piece of paper and he then announced: "Word has just been received that the rail strike has been settled on terms proposed by the President."

Strikes of 1951 and 1952. On August 25, 1950, President Truman ordered the Army to seize all railroads to prevent a general strike after unions had rejected the terms of an eighteen cents per hour raise for yardmen but none for trainmen. "Sick" switchmen struck the roads from January 31 to February 8, 1951, an action which cost their union $100,000 for striking in defiance of injunctions. On March 9, 1952, five thousand engineers, firemen, and conductors went on strike in the midwest in defiance of the Army's back-to-work appeal. On March 11 the government obtained a court order to end the work stoppage but five hundred strikers in Toledo and Elkhart remained out for another day. Finally, as peace returned to the nation's rails, the companies were returned to their owners on May 23.

Since that time there have been numerous strikes and scattered walk-outs, mostly for increased pay or in connection with the thorny problem of how to eliminate firemen no longer needed on certain diesel switching engines.

A major change in strike strategy took place in 1971.

Until that time railroads would not let the unions use the selective-strike weapon, which enables a union to close down one or a few selected companies at a time, thereby avoiding a national emergency but tieing up traffic regionally. Whenever the selective-strike was employed by the unions, the railroads retaliated by shutting down the entire industry. With a court decision in the spring of 1971 that permitted railroad unions to call selective-strikes, a whole new set of problems was created for dealing with walkouts on connecting or strategically located railroads.

(See also: American Railway Union; Eugene V. Debs; General Managers' Association; Railroad Labor Acts.)

REUTHER, WALTER PHILIP

Walter Reuther, longtime leader of the United Automobile Workers (UAW), was born in Wheeling, West Virginia, September 1, 1907. At sixteen he left Wheeling High School to help support the family and became a toolmaker's apprentice at The Wheeling Steel Company. Three years later Walter was fired when he tried to organize the men in a protest against having to work on Sunday. He went to Detroit, and after working a thirteen-hour night shift at Briggs Motors, took a job at Ford as a skilled toolmaker. At the same time he completed his high school education and then took economics and sociology courses at Wayne University. Here he was active in the radical student movement and in 1932 campaigned for Norman Thomas, the Socialist presidential candidate.

The next year he lost his job for trying to organize the Ford workers. After taking a trip abroad with his brother Victor, Walter joined the General Motors Ternstedt plant. He immediately started organizing the workers and was elected president of Local 174 of the UAW. A discharge and blacklisting were his reward, so he turned to the Kelsey Hayes Wheel factory where Victor was working and with his help called a sudden sit-down strike. In return for sending the men back to work Reuther was permitted to sign up the workers, this victory increasing Local 174's membership to thirty thousand.

The Reuther brothers were active in the General Motors sit-down strike of 1937, and Walter was involved in most of the other sit-down strikes of that period. Walter Reuther's fame spread after the 1937 "Battle of the Overpass" in which he, Richard Frankensteen, and other UAW leaders were beaten by Ford servicemen. In 1942 Reuther was elected vice president of the UAW and in 1946, after battling the Communist element in the union, became president.

During World War II Reuther served as a labor representative on the War Production Board and authored the "Reuther Plan" for mass producing airplanes in automobile factories. He abided by labor's wartime "no-strike" pledge, but once the war was over led a 113-day strike against General Motors in which he demanded "wage increases without price increases." Reuther argued that the size of the company's profits made this possible and that the pay increase would help sustain the nation's purchasing power.

Reuther, a neat and fastidious dresser, appeared more like a young industrialist than a labor leader. His intelligence could not be denied, nor his iron nerve and fierce loyalty to the union cause. An advocate of many far-reaching political and social reforms, he appeared before Congressional Committees to testify for better medical insurance and higher Social Security payments. He brought imagination to his job, built a powerful union, made his name stand for aggressive leadership and demonstrated ability to deal successfully with his union members. At the same time he developed prestige in the public eye.

In 1949 Reuther obtained medical insurance and pensions for the auto workers and three years later, on the death of Philip Murray, was elected president of the Congress of Industrial Organizations. As soon as the AFL-CIO merger took place in 1955 he became vice president, but when the UAW withdrew from the AFL-CIO in 1968, Reuther resigned and was reelected president of the auto workers' union. He thereupon worked out a partnership between the UAW and the International Brotherhood of Teamsters to form the Alliance for Labor Action. On May 9, 1970, Reuther died in an airplane crash near Pellston, Michigan.

(See also: Alliance for Labor Action; "Battle of the Overpass"; Richard Frankensteen; Sit-Down Strikes; United Automobile Workers.)

RIGHT TO WORK

The Wagner Act and the Taft-Hartley Act forbid discrimination "in regard to hire or tenure of employment or any term or condition of employment to encourage or discourage membership in any labor organization." Until these laws are amended or repealed, employers are not obligated to compel employees to join a union or lose their jobs. However, when collective bargaining results in a contract that requires compulsory unionism, both management and labor disregard the rights of the individual worker in this respect. Many states have right-to-work laws which make it illegal to require a worker to belong to a union in order to obtain or hold a job.

(See also: Right-to-Work Laws.)

RIGHT-TO-WORK LAWS

Those who object to compulsory unionism believe it is contrary to our American way of life to force a man to join any kind of organization and contribute to its financial support in order to obtain employment. The closed shop or compulsory unionism, they say, helps to create union monopoly.

A union that represents a majority of a company's employees understandably feels it is not fair for non-members to share all of the wage increases and other benefits which it has spent money to win. As a partial solution to the problem the "agency shop" was devised to obtain financial aid from non-union members, but of course any union would rather win a closed shop where it could represent every employee.

By 1972 nineteen states had enacted right-to-work laws which effectively barred the closed or union shop, preferential hiring, and maintenance of membership agreements between employers and unions.*

An advertisement of the South Carolina State Development Board stated in part: "Our average working week is 41.2 hours. And our 'right-to-work law' insures the right to work regardless of membership or non-membership in any organization. So consider locating in South Carolina. You'll be able to do business painlessly here."

A study based on U.S. Bureau of Labor statistics showed that states with right-to-work laws outstripped non-right-to-work states in the rate of industrial expansion, creation of new jobs, and rate of improvement in hourly wages, but there was no proof that the right-to-work laws were responsible. Another survey conducted by *Fortune* maga-

* The usual maintenance of membership clause in a contract requires that employees who belong to a union must maintain their membership until expiration of the union contract.

169

zine revealed that right-to-work laws have little effect on labor union membership.

RUNAWAY SHOP

Often a union makes wage demands which an employer is either unable or unwilling to grant. When this happens, and the employer closes the plant and moves his operation to another location in order to escape the union's jurisdiction, it is known as a runaway shop.

S ·······················

SABOTAGE

Sabotage is the term used when workers deliberately damage or destroy tools, equipment, or company property. It originated during the 1800's because French workingmen often threw their *sabots* or wooden shoes into the machinery to stop production when they were involved in a labor dispute. In the United States the Industrial Workers of the World urged workers to sabotage employers' property as part of their strategy to win a labor fight.

SCAB

Those who take jobs during a strike or continue to work for a company during a strike are known as scabs. Nonunion workers who pass through a picket line to accept employment are also called scabs. The term "scab" was in use as early as 1800.

"A 'scab' is to his trade what a traitor is to his country," Samuel Gompers, president of the American Federation of Labor, wrote in his *Seventy Years of Life and Labor*. "He is the first to take advantage of any benefit secured by union action, and never contributes anything toward its achievement."

Distinction should be made between a scab and a strikebreaker, who is also known in labor circles as a "fink" or "rat." Strikebreakers who are brought into a plant are usually hired through well established channels and leave their jobs as soon as the strike has been settled.

(See also: Strikebreaker.)

SEAMEN'S ACT

During the late nineteenth century, working conditions for the American seaman were deplorable. He was under the absolute command of the captain when at sea, he dared not quit his job for fear of being treated as a deserter, he could not join with fellow seamen to bargain for better pay or improved working conditions lest he be accused of mutiny. Furthermore, many sailors were kept in a perpetual condition of peonage by the "crimp"—a man who functioned as a boardinghouse keeper and employment agent. Between jobs a crimp would give the sailor board and keep and when his bill was large enough, obtain him a job. Then he forced the seaman to sign over several months' wages which were paid by the shipping company as soon as the ship had sailed.

Andrew Furuseth, a lobbyist for the Sailor's Union of the Pacific Coast, had little success in bringing about reforms until the Progressives made "seamen's liberties" one

171

of the principal issues in the 1912 Presidential campaign. Senator Robert M. La Follette later introduced a strong reform bill which was enacted in March, 1915, as the La Follette Seamen's Act.

The law abolished imprisonment for desertion in a safe harbor, gave sailors the right to obtain half their earned wages in any port, established standards for food allowances and living conditions, set a nine-hour day when in port, protected the seamen from abuse by crimps, made shipowners responsible for any corporal punishment administered at sea, and set new safety regulations.

SEATTLE GENERAL STRIKE

When shipyard workers in Seattle struck for higher wages in February, 1919, James A. Duncan, an aggressive radical who had been affiliated with the revolutionary Industrial Workers of the World, called a general strike of all workers. The industrial life of the city was practically paralyzed for five days, and citizens were unable to obtain most of their normal services as sixty thousand men stayed away from their jobs.

Although the strike was not important in itself, it created nationwide fear over the threat of Bolshevism, since the mayor had declared that this was a Bolshevist plot. Labor union leaders realized that it would be dangerous to join in such strikes because they would lose public sympathy or support.

Nevertheless, another such strike was called in San Francisco in July, 1934, when a quarrel between longshoremen and their employers grew into a general labor walkout of all industry and services. With the arrival of General Hugh Johnson who headed the National Recovery Administration, the one day general strike collapsed quickly.

Shaw, Lemuel

This highly regarded jurist and chief justice of the Massachusetts Supreme Judicial Court was born in Barnstable, Massachusetts on January 9, 1781, and took his legal training at Harvard University. The attorney served in the Massachusetts legislature both as a representative and senator and wrote Boston's first city charter. Shaw sat as chief justice in the Supreme Judicial Court from 1830–1860 and died in Boston on March 30, 1861.

Chief Justice Shaw wrote more than two thousand opinions, many of which are still cited by attorneys. He became famous because he did not hesitate to set legal precedents in cases involving economic and social changes created by the industrial revolution, this being a field in which there were few if any precedents to draw upon. His most famous decision was in the case of *Commonwealth v. Hunt,* a milestone decision which held that it was not a criminal act for a combination of employees or a union to refuse to work for an employer who hires nonunion labor. The old common law conspiracy doctrine did not apply to labor unions thus declaring the legality of such organizations and their right to strike for higher wages.

Sit-Down Strikes

A sit-down strike is one in which workers remain within the plant and force it to close.

In 1936, when leaders of the United Automobile Workers (UAW) were trying to win recognition for their union with the General Motors Corporation, the union members at the Cleveland Fisher Body Plant decided to halt production on December 28 and refused to work or leave their posts. The next day when five union men requested collective bargaining and were fired from the Flint, Michigan, Fisher Body No. 2 Plant, the men sat down at their machines. The larger Fisher Body Plant in Flint was next to have its sit-downers after they discovered that the management was taking the dies out at night. By New Year's Day the men were firmly settled in the two Flint plants, and soon other General Motors facilities were forced to close for lack of parts. The sit-downers remained in the plants for forty-four days until the company and the UAW signed an agreement in which the union was recognized as the bargaining agency for its members.

Immediately sit-down strikes spread rapidly, affecting even the Woolworth stores where the clerks stood defiantly behind counters refusing to wait on customers. However, the sit-down strategy was soon abandoned, and in February 1939, the Supreme Court decided that such strikes were illegal and that an employer had the right to discharge employees who adopted this tactic.

SOCIAL SECURITY

At the depths of the Depression of the 1930's, President Franklin D. Roosevelt appointed a Committee on Economic Security to prepare a program of "greater economic security" and submit its report to him by January 1, 1935. In August of that year Congress adopted the Social Security Act which established a national insurance program and an agency, the Social Security Administration, to administer it. The original law has been amended to increase benefits and broaden the types of assistance which include the following:

(1) Unemployment insurance for workers who have been unemployed or released from work for more than a week. This is administered by the states and financed by a special payroll tax.

(2) Old age retirement insurance administered by the federal Social Security Administration and financed by

174

contributions from employers, employees, and the federal government.

(3) Workmen's compensation or disability insurance for those who are disabled by industrial injuries or diseases and unable to work for even as short a time as a year.

(4) Hospitalization insurance for those over sixty-five, this program being known as Medicare.

(5) Supplementary medical insurance for those over sixty-five to cover payment of doctors' and related bills, costs shared by the insured and the federal government. This is a voluntary plan known as Medicaid.

(6) Assistance to the blind, needy, aged, and needy families with children who are deprived of parental support. The states receive matching grants-in-aid to help pay for this.

(7) Aid to crippled, needy, and dependent children.

(8) Aid to those who have become permanently disabled.

(9) Vocational and health programs.

(See also: Unemployment Insurance.)

SOCIALIST LABOR PARTY

Organized originally on July 4, 1874, as the Social Democratic Workingmen's Party of the United States, the founders adopted a vague socialist platform. In 1877 they changed the name to Socialist Labor Party (SLP) and became the first nationwide socialist political organization.

The SLP elected some minor officials in several states but further success was doomed when Daniel De Leon joined in 1890 and thereafter dominated the party. He expounded his beliefs in Marxism, advocated the overthrow of capitalism, and opposed the leaders of organized labor. The party achieved some success in the elections of 1898 but thereafter its popularity declined rapidly.

175

Socialist Party

In 1899 the SLP split when Morris Hillquit persuaded a group of members to join up with the midwestern Socialists who, the following year, nominated Eugene V. Debs for president. In 1901 these moderates from the SLP helped found the Socialist Party. Since that time the SLP has practically disappeared from view although it has run candidates in every Presidential election.

(See also: Eugene V. Debs; Daniel De Leon; Socialist Party.)

SOCIALIST PARTY

In 1897 Eugene V. Debs, Victor L. Berger, and others organized the Social Democratic Party of America. The next year a group split off to form the Social Democratic Party which achieved some success in local and state elections. In 1901 at a Unity Conference, Berger, Debs, and their followers joined with the group of moderates from the Socialist Labor Party to form the Socialist Party. From that time until 1920 Debs ran as its presidential candidate and the party's membership grew to 118,045 in 1912. That same year Socialist mayors were elected in fifty-six cities and another thousand Socialists held public offices in various cities and states.

The year 1912 represented the party's peak membership. During the following year internal fighting broke out over communism, war, syndicalist tactics, and other issues. Nevertheless, the party drew 919,799 votes in the 1920 presidential election.* After Debs' death in 1926 Norman Thomas, a former minister and writer, ran as the party's presidential candidate from 1928 through 1948.

---

* This was the greatest number of votes the party ever won in spite of the fact that Debs was serving a term in the Atlanta Penitentiary on a war-time espionage charge for making an anti-war speech in Canton, Ohio.

176

The party has tried to win the support of other groups to establish socialism in America through evolutionary rather than revolutionary means. It has backed many reform programs, including housing and welfare legislation, social security, better labor conditions, and expanded control over business. Thomas became discouraged over the party's failure to win more support at the polls and advocated abandoning political activities in favor of education. Other party leaders did not agree, but during the 1950's the Socialists emphasized education rather than election of their candidates to public office. In 1952 Thomas organized the Union for Democratic Socialism to function as an educational organization.

In 1948, the last election in which Norman Thomas ran for president, he polled a total of 139,572 votes. In 1956, the most recent year the Socialist Party has run a presidential candidate, it polled a total of 2,126 votes.

(See also: Victor L. Berger; Eugene V. Debs; Socialist Labor Party.)

Steel Industry Strikes

Because of the importance of steel as a basic product for industry, a prolonged steel strike can have serious effects on the nation's economy. Lack of the metal can cause certain industries to close, and the size of pay awards granted steelworkers often sets the level which other unions seek in their bargaining for improved wages. As in the case of all strike articles in this book only major work stoppages are covered.

Homestead Strike of 1892. (See Homestead Strike.)

Strike of 1901. The formation of the United States Steel Corporation (U.S. Steel) in 1900 created a serious problem for the Amalgamated Association of Iron, Steel, and Tin Workers (Amalgamated) which had been organized among the skilled steel workers in 1876. The leaders realized that this new company which was only partially unionized could pit union steel mills against nonunion companies and effectively wipe out unionism in the entire industry.

In 1901 representatives of the Amalgamated met with executives of several divisions of the new company to demand increased wages and that all the mills be unionized. The officers replied that they would adopt union wages for all the unionized and some of the nonunionized mills, but that none of the plants would recognize the union as a bargaining agent for their employees. Immediately the Amalgamated called 46,000 members out on strike. The new company was in no financial position to accept a strike, however, and agreed to grant the union wage demands to most but not all of their employees. Thereupon 16,000 additional men stayed away from their jobs.

Unfortunately for the Amalgamated, it had not won the backing of the unskilled workers who had either remained at work or returned to their jobs after a few "vacation" days. U.S. Steel brought in strikebreakers, reopened the mills, and forced the union to concede defeat. Although its wage demands were granted, the Amalgamated had to promise that it would not attempt to organize steelworkers, that its members would work alongside nonunion men, and that the company could fire anyone engaging in union activities.

Strike of 1909. During 1902 U.S. Steel instituted a profit sharing program aimed chiefly at unskilled, low-paid workers and subsequently gave them other benefits. By 1908 the sheet and tin plate division had the only unionized mills in the company; the following June U.S. Steel announced that thereafter it would operate an open shop everywhere.

178

The Amalgamated lost no time calling a strike and this time even the nonunion workers responded. They believed that the benefits they had received were prompted by the company's fear of the union. All but one mill shut down and in some plants the strike lasted for more than a year. U.S. Steel obtained injunctions against picketing at some plants, brought in strikebreakers, and in many places harassed the strikers badly. After a month, the mills which were not unionized resumed operation, and no effort was made to settle the strike elsewhere. In November the American Federation of Labor sent financial help to the strikers but this did not save the union cause. In March, 1910, U.S. Steel instituted a higher wage scale, whereupon the strikers abandoned their picket lines and returned to their jobs. At the same time the union acknowledged that the corporation had become an open shop. Thereafter, the Amalgamated became a small craft union which was not involved with the mass of unskilled workers.

Strike of 1919. In 1918 William Z. Foster, an ex-member of the radical Industrial Workers of the World, led a group of American Federation of Labor leaders in forming the National Committee for the Organizing of the Iron and Steel Industry. As a result of the Committee's activities, the companies conceded some wage and hour improvements and by May, 1919, the Committee had signed up a hundred thousand men. The Committee then announced a number of demands including a living wage, double pay for overtime, and abolition of company unions. The corporations refused to grant the requests and on September 22 over 350,000 workers left their jobs.

The steel companies waged a vicious war against the strikers, eighteen of whom were killed during the strike. The employers were aided by the antiunion press which

179

called the steel workers dangerous Bolshevists and painted a completely erroneous picture of the workers. Within two months of the strike call enough Negro strikebreakers and company spies had been hired to restore 75 percent of the normal production. By the first part of January, 1920, the union was forced to cancel the strike. This defeat postponed organization of the steelworkers for another eighteen years.

"Little Steel" Strike of 1937. (See "Little Steel" Strike.)

Strike of 1952. In April of 1952 the Wage Stabilization Board recommended to steel managements a fifteen cent an hour wage increase to enable steelworkers to catch up with other unions and the cost of living. It also recommended a union shop. The companies rejected the proposal, whereupon the steelworkers prepared to strike. Before the men walked out, President Harry Truman ordered the government to seize the mills and put the Wage Stabilization Board proposals into effect. The following month a court ruled that the President had acted illegally and the decision was upheld by the Supreme Court. The President then returned the mills to their owners and a fifty-three day strike resulted. Finally the union and the industry agreed on a sixteen cent wage increase and a union shop compromise agreement.

Strike of 1959. After heeding an appeal by President Dwight Eisenhower to postpone for two weeks its proposed strike for higher wages, the United Steelworkers of America started its sixth walkout since World War II on July 15, 1959. With 500,000 workers out, 85 percent of the nation's steel production was halted. Negotiations dragged along without making any progress, and by October 7 more than 225,000 workers in non-steel industries had been laid off due to the lack of metal. President Eisenhower invoked the Taft-Hartley Act that day and created an inquiry board which reported on the 19th that accord appeared impossible.

On the President's orders an eighty-day Taft-Hartley anti-strike injunction was issued by a U.S. district judge because continuation of the strike would imperil the national health and safety. An hour later the U.S. 3rd Circuit Court of Appeals stayed the order. Industry-union negotiations resumed, and on October 26 Kaiser Steel Corp. signed an agreement with the union after which two other small companies also capitulated.

Meanwhile the strike continued elsewhere, but on November 7 the Supreme Court upheld the Taft-Hartley injunction, thus halting the longest nationwide steel strike in its 116th day. The men returned to work but the union planned to renew the strike after the eighty days cooling off period. Suddenly, on January 5, 1960, final settlement of the strike was announced. The steel industry feared that the government might force them to accept an unsatisfactory agreement and therefore gave in to the union. This constituted a victory for organized labor as a whole because it showed how much economic power it had when it stood up and defended the interests of its membership.

STRIKEBREAKER

A strikebreaker is someone who is not a regular employee of a company but accepts a job with that company when the regular workers are on strike. The purpose of strikebreaking, for the most part, has always been to destroy a union. Three principal methods have been used to achieve this goal: (1) private police or guards are brought into a plant to intimidate workers who are eager to go out on strike; (2) professional strikebreakers are hired to replace strikers; (3) companies promote a "back to work

181

movement" among the strikers and their families in order to break down the striker's morale.

(See also: Scab.)

SWEATSHOP

Places of business, where employees were forced to work for low wages, very long hours, and under conditions which were below accepted standards, were known as sweatshops.

Sweatshops were prevalent in large cities before the turn of this century. They sprang up partly because of the large number of immigrants who were mostly unskilled and therefore forced to accept whatever employment might be offered. Two other conditions which contributed to the sweatshop system were the ability of owners to contract for the work on a piece basis, and the availability of inexpensive machinery. This enabled a man who had a minimum of capital to set up shop and to profit from the cheaper labor market. A suitmaker, for example, needed only to rent a loft and purchase the cloth to be made up into suits. In many of these shops employees had to bring their own sewing machines, scissors, and thread.

The sweatshops were forced to close when workers became organized and insisted on better wages, hours, and working conditions, and when social legislation required sweatshop employers to improve their shops. The cost of doing this made it impossible for most of them to survive. Some of the most notorious sweatshops were found in the New York City garment industry.

T ••

TAFT-HARTLEY ACT

Following World War II, as the nation was readjusting to a peacetime economy, many people felt that the unions had become too powerful under the Wagner Act and that labor laws should be revised. Business was concerned about its lack of bargaining power, union coercion of its employees, damaging jurisdictional strikes and boycotts, breaking of agreements, and other abuses, and felt that management should be permitted to "manage" its employees. Congress adopted the Labor-Management Relations Act, better known as the Taft-Hartley Act. "Shocking—bad for labor, bad for management, bad for the country," was President Harry Truman's description of the bill. Despite his veto, Congress passed it a second time and it became law on June 23, 1947.

The act was far-reaching and represented a compromise between what labor's foes wanted and what its friends would concede. The most important provisions included the following:

It allowed employers to sue unions for breach of contract; provided for "cooling off" periods and presidential use of eighty-day injunctions in strikes that imperiled national health and safety; prohibited closed and preferential shops and union hiring halls; permitted union shops only on a vote of a majority of the employees; * forbade union contributions to national elections or primaries;

* An amendment adopted October 22, 1951, permitted union shop contracts without voting permission of employees.

183

forbade secondary boycotts * and jurisdictional strikes; guaranteed employers the right to express opinions on unions without reprisal or use of force against their employees; forbade employers to contribute to health and welfare funds unless they were administered by a board of trustees on which employers and employees were represented; exempted employers from bargaining with unions of supervisors or foremen unless they chose to do so; and restricted many unfair union practices.

The National Labor Relations Board (NLRB) was enlarged to five members and a Presidentially appointed general counsel was added to handle the prosecution of unfair labor practices. Henceforth services of the NLRB were to be available only to those unions which filed certain financial reports with the Secretary of Labor and distributed them to their own members. Finally, each official of a national or international union had to file an affidavit stating he was not a Communist. This non-Communist oath was upheld by the Supreme Court on May 8, 1950.

As expected, most labor leaders denounced the law and John L. Lewis refused to sign the non-Communist oath. There is no evidence that unions have been unduly hurt by the law. Some amendments were subsequently adopted which favored unions, while others tightened some of the provisions pertaining to union activities.

(See also: Landrum-Griffin Act; National Labor Relations Board.)

TEAMSTERS' UNION

The International Brotherhood of Teamsters, Chauffeurs, Warehousemen, and Helpers of America, is better

* The Landrum-Griffin Act of 1959 amended the Taft-Hartley Act with respect to boycotts and picketing to limit even further the economic power of unions.

known as the Teamsters and is the largest labor union in the country. Founded in 1899 to unionize the drivers of horse-pulled vehicles, it was at first called the Team Drivers International Union. From 1907 until 1952 Daniel J. Tobin served as president and increased the membership during his term of office from 40,000 to 1,100,000. When he left office the union was worth $30,000,000 and had become a major power in the American Federation of Labor (AFL).

Tobin believed in craft unionism and strongly supported the AFL. When John L. Lewis organized the Congress of Industrial Organizations, he tried to argue Tobin into joining his federation, but Tobin stuck by his belief in separating workers by occupations and remained within the AFL. Thereafter the Teamsters and CIO were constantly raiding each other's memberships.

James Hoffa joined the union in 1932 and opposed Tobin's insistence on adhering to the crafts as well as his lack of aggressiveness in expanding the membership. This issue caused dissension within the union between David Beck and Hoffa on the one hand, and Tobin on the other. Beck and Hoffa were strong regional leaders in the west and central states. In 1937 Beck organized an eleven-state Western Conference, and after becoming president in 1953, he set up conferences for the rest of the country.

In 1957 Senator John L. McClellan headed a committee whose purpose was to investigate union officials suspected of corrupt practices. He subsequently denounced Beck and Hoffa as leaders of a "racket-ridden, gangster infested, and scandal packed" union. As a result of the hearings, the AFL-CIO expelled the Teamsters, and Beck went to jail on charges of income-tax evasion and larceny. Hoffa took his place and changed the union into a strong centralized organization, but in 1967 he, too, went to prison for tampering with a jury. He was released in 1971 with the proviso that he could not engage in the direct or indirect management of any labor organization until March 6, 1980. The Teamsters joined with the United Automobile Workers in 1968 to form the Alliance for Labor Action.

(See also: Alliance for Labor Action; David Beck; James Hoffa.)

TEXTILE STRIKE OF 1934

On August 27, 1934, representatives of the cotton garment industry adopted a resolution stating their intention to ignore the NRA Code which had been established for their industry under the National Recovery Act. Some of the provisions of the code provided for reduction of hours of labor and a minimum hourly wage. The manufacturers called them "unjustifiable, unwarranted, burdensome and inequitable."

The United Textile Workers responded four days later by telling a million employees to strike the cotton, wool and silk industries. The strike would be cancelled when the employers recognized the union, abolished the speedup and stretch-out,* and instituted a thirty-hour workweek without reducing the minimum fourteen dollar a week wage. The union was not impressed by the fact that the industry had been economically depressed for some time. This did not excuse the industrialists from disobeying the textile code.

Within a few days a half-million textile workers were

* The term "speedup" refers to any acceleration in work or output which is demanded by an employer who may or may not pay additional wages for the increased production. A "stretchout" is any system which requires employees to do more work but without any increase in pay. A "slowdown" in production may be called by employees (1) to make the work last longer, or (2) to reduce the plant's output when there is a labor dispute.

on strike, making this the largest national strike in the nation's history. The union dispatched "flying squadrons" to go from one southern town to another to sign up members and incite textile workers to strike and set up picket lines. Violence was so widespread that eight governors called out the National Guard to preserve order. Governor Francis Green of Rhode Island asked the legislature to request federal troops to assist the guardsmen. "We are face to face now not with a textile strike," he said, "but with a Communist uprising." The legislature did not agree, and after Green talked with President Roosevelt he decided that the crisis had passed.

On September 21 the union recalled the strikers to work after the President appointed a committee headed by Governor John Winant of New Hampshire to study the problem and issue its recommendations. The committee's "peace treaty" made several suggestions but left the basic issues unresolved, and the textile workers were forced to accept the same working conditions that just three weeks earlier they had asserted were intolerable.

After the union revoked the strike call, about 200 mills remained closed in the South and 80,000 workers lost their jobs. In some New England plants, employers discriminated against the strikers, refusing to rehire them. Many employers who had tried previously to help provide additional employment for textile workers decided not to reopen their mills.

Half-a-million workers had sacrificed up to three weeks' wages, thousands lost their jobs, and several hundred thousand men and women who had joined the United Textile Workers during the strike tore up their union cards in disgust. For the time being the textile workers saw no hope of bettering either wages or working conditions.

187

THIRTY HOUR WEEK

During the early 1930's when the country was in the throes of a depression, Senator Hugo Black introduced a bill providing for a thirty hour week. The purpose was to stimulate economic recovery by making more jobs available since people would only work six hours a day, five days a week. The bill passed the Senate in April 1933, but failed in the House.

Exactly thirty years later, labor leaders wanted to solve the unemployment problem by instituting the thirty-five hour week with no reduction in wages. The AFL-CIO admitted that the thirty-five hour workweek was not a cure-all but a tool to help combat unemployment. The real intent of the drive was to goad the Administration into adopting some kind of economic program that would create jobs. Nevertheless, trade unions have been working to shorten the standard workweek from forty to thirty-five hours because reduction of hours of work has always been a goal of workers and unions.

Business offered an alternate solution to the thirty-five hour workweek as a means of solving unemployment. It claimed that the way to put people to work was to expand the economy and encourage industry to invest more money in plants and equipment in order to create more jobs.

One alternate means of providing workers longer periods of leisure time is the four day week which was gaining some acceptance during the early 1970's. By working a ten hour day Monday through Thursday instead of forty hours for five days employees would enjoy a three day weekend. Similarly, those who had gained a thirty-five hour week would be at their jobs almost nine hours a day in order to gain the weekly holiday.

TOMPKINS SQUARE RIOT

The Panic of 1873 caused widespread unemployment and misery among workingmen, most of whom had no savings to fall back upon or other sources of financial aid. Usually, whenever these unemployed men and women gathered in public places to protest their lot, police broke up the meetings. Often the men fought back, maintaining they had the right of free assembly.

On January 13, 1874, another such meeting was scheduled to be held in New York City's Tompkins Square. Workers who could not find jobs wanted to show the city their need for some kind of relief. The mayor promised to address the group, but when it was found that radical members of the American branch of the International Workingmen's Association had assisted in arranging for the gathering, the police permit for the meeting was cancelled at the last minute.

Those who planned to attend the rally knew nothing of the cancellation and filled the square. As they waited for the program to start, suddenly, without warning, mounted police appeared and charged into the crowd indiscriminately, clubbing everyone who came within their reach. Men, women, and children were knocked to the ground and many were trampled by the horses. Even bystanders who were watching from a distance were hurt as they tried to escape from the rampaging police.

The New York *Times* ascribed the riot to a mob of foreigners, mostly Irishmen or Germans, and called the demonstration the work of alien radicals. One participant, who escaped injury by jumping into a cellarway, later wrote in his autobiography:

"I saw how professions of radicalism and sensationalism concentrated all the forces of society against a labor movement and nullified in advance a normal, necessary activity.

189

I saw that leadership in the labor movement could be safely entrusted only to those into whose hearts and minds had been woven the experience of earning their bread by daily labor. I saw that betterment for workingmen must come primarily through workingmen. . . ." *

Samuel Gompers, the author of these words, was only twenty-four at the time, but no doubt the experience reenforced his determination to devote his life to the union cause.

TRADE SOCIETIES

During the latter part of the eighteenth century the various journeymen who lived in the American Colonies began to form local trade societies. These groups had no intention of pressing for economic gain but were essentially mutual aid or philanthropic societies which were organized to provide sick and death benefits for their members. In larger cities many of the leading trades had established these groups by 1790. In some states local societies banded together into larger organizations such as the Albany Mechanics' Society, the Association of Mechanics of the Commonwealth of Massachusetts, and the General Society of Mechanics and Tradesmen in New York.

The societies reflected the pride and independence of the workers who preferred to provide for their own needs rather than have to apply for public or private charity. Many of the trade societies had their own meeting halls which were also used for social functions.

Although trade unions were a natural outgrowth of the early trade societies, as stated above, the original purpose of these groups was mutual protection rather than eco-

* Samuel Gompers: *Seventy Years of Life and Labor.*

190

nomic gain. The New York Society of Journeymen Shipwrights was organized with the understanding that the society would be dissolved if members made any attempts to set wages. It was natural, however, that these organizations which represented skilled workmen would gradually broaden their scope to represent their members in economic disputes with employers and thus become small craft unions.

TRADE UNION

A trade union is an organization formed by workers in a craft or trade who wish to promote their common interests and welfare by negotiating as a group with their employer for improved wages, shorter hours, and other working conditions.

TRIANGLE SHIRTWAIST FACTORY FIRE

One of the most tragic fires in our nation's history occurred on New York City's East Side on March 25, 1911, when a fire broke out on the eighth floor and swept up through a multistory loft building. Employees of the Triangle Shirtwaist Factory worked in their sweatshop on the top three floors. The exit door was locked and two other doors which opened inward could not be used because the frenzied employees crowded behind them. This prevented the women from opening the doors to reach the stairway and thus escape from the burning building. Some of the trapped workers burned to death within the building, others panicked and jumped from the ninth floor windows to their death several hundred feet below on the cobblestone street.

The disaster, which took 146 lives, helped focus attention on the need for changing old laws, revising building codes, enforcing safety regulations in factories, and providing more severe punishment for violations.

U

UNEMPLOYMENT

Every worker dreams of job security and for good reason. Business recessions and depressions can mean widespread layoffs for thousands or even fifteen million men and women, as was the case in 1933 when President Franklin D. Roosevelt took office and promised to help the unemployed and destitute. The New Deal administration set the precedent that henceforth government would provide jobs during periods of widespread unemployment.

In the Employment Act of 1946, Congress stated: "The Congress declares that it is the continuing policy and responsibility of the Federal Government to use all practical means . . . for the purpose of creating and maintaining . . . conditions under which there will be afforded useful employment opportunities . . . for those able, willing and seeking to work, and to promote maximum employment, production, and purchasing power."

Since World War II the labor force has grown steadily, but the percent of the civilian labor force which has been unemployed has varied from time to time as shown in the following table:

192

Year	Unemployment Rate
1955	4.4%
1960	5.5
1965	4.5
1970	4.9
1971 (April)	5.7
1972 (April)	5.9

There is always some unemployment due to seasonal layoffs when resorts close, construction is halted, or various agricultural jobs are no longer available. There is unemployment because some workers are changing jobs, others are temporarily or permanently disabled. Technological changes and automation create unemployment, too, but automation never caused the mass layoffs which were feared.

A worker may be out of work for other reasons. He may be a member of a minority race against which discrimination is practiced; he may have no skills to offer an employer; he may be living in a depressed area where there is no industry; he may have mental or physical handicaps; he may have a skill which has become obsolete and therefore needs retraining.

The main goal of every economy should be to keep men and machines busy and to provide a job for everyone who wants to work. Actually there is no such thing as full employment for the reasons outlined above, and economists therefore believe that if only three or four percent of the labor force is unemployed we have a satisfactory situation.

UNEMPLOYMENT INSURANCE

Under the Social Security Act of 1935 a program of unemployment insurance was established to be administered by the states and financed by a special payroll tax borne by employers. In most states the standard rate is 2.7 percent of taxable payroll, but employers whose records show that their business has had little unemployment receive lower rates as a reward. In 1971 the estimated average rate for employers was 1.5 percent and effective July 1, 1972 the tax was made payable only on the first $4,200 of a worker's pay except in Minnesota where the limit is $4,800; in Hawaii, $6,000; and in Alaska, $7,200. In a few states employees also participate by giving a small percentage of money under certain circumstances.

Employers contribute to the federal government an additional 0.5 percent of the first $4,200 paid each employee. This money supports the state and federal costs of administering the federal security program of unemployment insurance and the nationwide employment service.

Although laws vary from state to state, usually after a waiting period of one week an unemployed person can start receiving insurance payments if he has been working for a certain length of time. He must not have been fired for misconduct or quit without good cause; he must not be involved in a labor dispute (although this is not true in all states); and he must be ready and willing to work. If he refuses a suitable position which is offered him at his local state employment office, he may lose further unemployment payments.

Each of the states operates employment offices which are affiliated with the United States Training and Employment Service. This agency has wide duties which include giving assistance in establishing and maintaining a system of public employment offices in all states and territories. It helps the various state employment agencies by providing techniques and data related to job development, placement, occupational analysis, job modification, counseling, and testing, as well as in many other ways, all of which have one purpose: to reduce unemployment.

(See also: Social Security.)

Union Label

Many unions place their trademarks (which have been registered with the Copyright Office) directly on each article, or on labels attached to their products, to show that the goods were manufactured by union members. The purpose of union labels is to encourage wider use of union-made articles.

Union labels first appeared in California during the 1870's when large numbers of Chinese workers were arriving and working for low wages. Unions became concerned and decided to use the labels in order to identify their products.

Union Membership

In 1971 union membership was at a record high, but it had not kept up with the growth of the work force. Between 1935 and 1970 union membership shot up more than five-fold from 3,500,000 to 19,400,000. This increase is not as impressive, however, when one considers the following table:

Year	Union Membership as a Percentage of all but Farm Employees
1950	31.5%
1955	33.2
1960	31.4
1965	28.4
1970	27.4

One explanation for the drop in union membership as a percentage of all but farm employees is that the various groups of workers which unions have been organizing have been growing smaller as more and more of them sign up with unions. This has left the white-collar employees as one of the largest segments of the labor force to be organized. Success has been achieved principally among government workers. Office workers in industry have traditionally resisted unionization because they are unwilling

	1960 Membership	1971 Membership	Change (%)	
Teamsters	1,484,400	2,020,000	Up	36%
Auto Workers	1,136,000	1,350,000	Up	19
Steelworkers	1,152,000	1,200,000	Up	4
Brotherhood of Electrical Workers	771,000	977,295	Up	27
Machinists	898,100	900,000	Up	0.2
Carpenters	800,000	808,000	Up	1
Laborers	442,500	650,000	Up	47
Retail Clerks	342,000	650,000	Up	90
Meat Cutters *	436,000	550,000	Up	26
State, County, Municipal Employees	210,000	525,000	Up	150
Communications Workers	259,900	500,000	Up	92
Service Employees	272,000	480,000	Up	76
Hotel, Restaurant Employees	443,000	450,000	Up	2
Ladies' Garment Workers	446,600	442,300	Down	1
Operating Engineers	291,000	400,000	Up	37

* Meat Cutters figures include those for former Packinghouse Workers Union, now merged.

SOURCE: 1960 figures, U.S. Department of Labor; 1971 figures, union sources as reported to *U.S. News & World Report*. Reprinted from *U.S. News & World Report*, Copyright 1972 U.S. News & World Report, Inc.

to pay dues or go out on strike. Many white-collar workers receive raises when unionized employees win increases, or they find that management may give them pay raises voluntarily in order to keep them from joining unions.

The preceding table shows the membership growth of the nation's fifteen largest labor unions. It can be seen that the state, county, and municipal employees constitute the fastest growing segment, with the Communications Workers and Retail Clerks in second and third place respectively.

Union Monopoly

The usual meaning of this term refers to the absolute power that a large union may have over an industry— when, for example, the Teamsters' Union calls a strike and has a monopolistic power or control over all the workers in the trucking industry.

A closed shop is sometimes referred to as a union monopoly since the union may be able to control how much labor is available through a slowdown or strike call, especially when it is bargaining for wages and working conditions.

Union Shop

Where a union shop is in effect, an employer is free to hire union or nonunion workers; but all new employees must join the union within a certain time limit, usually thirty days. Each such employee must also continue to pay dues to the union for the duration of the union contract.

Unions have been concerned when not all employees are required to belong to a union which is acting as the bargaining agency for the organized workers. The "free riders," as such nonunion employees are known, reap all of the benefits won by the union without having to pay their share of the union costs.

In an agency shop nonunion employees are not required to join the union, but they must pay dues or service charges to the bargaining agent which was selected by the unionized employees. In 1963 the Supreme Court decided that the agency shop is legal under the Taft-Hartley Act.

(See also: Closed Shop; Open Shop.)

United Automobile Workers

The official name of this union is the International Union, United Automobile, Aerospace and Agricultural Implement Workers of America. The Automobile Workers Union was formed in 1935 to take the place of the National Council of Automobile Workers which was affiliated with the American Federation of Labor. It withdrew from the AFL the following year, and under the leadership of its new president, Homer Martin, became the United Automobile Workers (UAW) and joined the Committee of Industrial Organization.

Following the sit-down strikes in General Motors' plants in Flint, Michigan, during 1937 and the subsequent recognition of the UAW by General Motors, the union grew rapidly. Later it signed contracts with Chrysler and Ford which made the UAW the bargaining agent for the Big Three automobile companies. Walter Reuther became vice president of the UAW in 1942 and served as president from 1946 until his death in 1970. In 1968 the UAW withdrew from the AFL-CIO and with the International Brotherhood of Teamsters formed the Alliance for Labor Action.

(See also: Alliance for Labor Action; Walter Reuther; Sit-Down Strikes.)

UNITED BROTHERHOOD OF CARPENTERS
AND JOINERS OF AMERICA

On August 8, 1881, delegates from fourteen local unions in eleven cities met in Chicago and established The Brotherhood of Carpenters and Joiners of America. The new union grew rapidly and aided in the formation of the American Federation of Labor (AFL) in 1886. During its early days the Carpenters fought for the eight-hour day, but it was not until 1907 that they had won this shorter work day on a comprehensive basis.

Under the leadership of William L. Hutcheson, who served as its president from 1915–1951, the union took an active part in fighting the American Plan and open shop movement in the 1920's. Hutcheson made the union one of the strongest in the nation, its constitution permitting him "to issue charters to auxiliary unions composed of persons working at an industry where organization would be a benefit to the brotherhood." As a result, the union was constantly involved in a stream of jurisdictional disputes, the most serious being with the International Association of Machinists.

In 1935 the AFL granted the Carpenters jurisdiction over the logging and lumber camps. Two years later, a number of logging locals in the Pacific Northwest resigned in disgust from the union because they could not participate in its affairs. They formed the International Woodworkers' Union, and affiliated with the CIO. Hutcheson lost no time crushing the new union which he did easily by instructing his members not to handle CIO wood and asking the Teamsters' Union to do the same. It was not long before thousands of the woodworkers had lost their jobs and had no choice but to abandon the CIO and return to the old union.

At the beginning of the 1970's the union's membership

199

stood at approximately 800,000. Maurice A. Hutcheson, born in 1897, was still at the helm, having succeeded his father in 1951.

UNITED MINE WORKERS OF AMERICA

The United Mine Workers of America (UMW) was the result of the merger, in 1890, of two unions which previously had organized miners in the bituminous coal fields. The new organization affiliated with the American Federation of Labor (AFL) but was unsuccessful in its organizing attempts until seven years later. In 1898 the UMW won an eight-hour day in four states.

Following strikes called in 1900 and 1902, the latter lasting six months and requiring intervention by President Theodore Roosevelt, the union became well entrenched in the anthracite coal mines. Under the direction of John Mitchell, the union won wide recognition and grew from 33,000 to 260,000 members during the ten years he served the UMW from 1897–1907.

Competition from nonunionized coal fields in West Virginia and Kentucky weakened the mines in the unionized northern states, and the power of the union gradually diminished during the 1920's and early 1930's. Nevertheless, John L. Lewis, UMW president from 1919–1960 and one of the nation's most aggressive labor leaders, fought steadily for his miners. Under the New Deal Lewis was able to organize the southern fields and reestablish the union's strength in the north.

The UMW was one of the first affiliates of the newly organized Committee for Industrial Organization which Lewis helped form in 1935. This group changed its name to Congress of Industrial Organizations (CIO) in 1937 and withdrew from the AFL. The UMW left the CIO in 1942 and returned to the AFL in 1946, but Lewis took his miners out again the following year. Thereafter the UMW has remained as an independent union.

During the 1940's the UMW was involved in repeated strikes both during and after World War II. These involved government seizure, walkouts in violation of court injunctions, and heavy fines imposed on both the union and John L. Lewis. The second half of this century has been marked by improved relations between the mine owners and the union and their ability to negotiate contracts amicably. The UMW has won many gains for its members including pensions and comprehensive medical benefits.

(See also: Coal Strikes; Congress of Industrial Organizations; John L. Lewis; John Mitchell.)

UNITED STATES DEPARTMENT OF LABOR

This executive department of the United States Government originally was part of the Department of Commerce and Labor (1903–1913). It was established by Congress on March 4, 1913, and is headed by a Secretary who is a member of the President's cabinet. The Department is responsible for administering and enforcing laws designed to advance the public interest by promoting the welfare of wage earners, improving their working conditions, and advancing their opportunities for profitable employment. The department has four main areas of interest: employment security, labor standards, manpower development and training, and international labor affairs.

Departmental activities are varied. They range from administering federal laws on minimum wages, working hours and public contracts; administering public employment service and unemployment insurance programs; serving as the government's chief fact-finding agency in labor economics; to developing apprenticeship standards for training skilled workers, promoting industrial safety, or administering laws covering the election of labor union officers. For a comprehensive and authoritative description of the department's responsibilities and activities see the current edition of the United States Government Organization Manual.

UNITED STEELWORKERS OF AMERICA

The Amalgamated Association of Iron, Steel and Tin Workers was organized in 1878 essentially as a craft union for skilled workers in the steel industry. After several disastrous steel strikes, the union became moribund in the 1920's, leaving the bulk of the steel workers with no representation. The failure of the American Federation of Labor to organize the steel industry gave its rebel Committee on Industrial Organization opportunity to do so. After working out an agreement with the Amalgamated Association, the Committee on Industrial Organization financed establishment of the Steel Workers Organizing Committee (SWOC) in 1936. The following year the SWOC signed an agreement with the United States Steel Corporation in which the new union was recognized as the bargaining agency for its members.

Following the SWOC's victory over the "Little Steel" companies, the union expanded its membership considerably and changed its name in 1942 to the United Steelworkers of America, thereby becoming an international union and affiliate of the Congress of Industrial Organizations. Philip Murray, who had served as chairman of the SWOC, was elected president, and on his death in 1952 was succeeded by David J. McDonald. In 1967 the International Union of Mine, Mill and Smelter Workers was merged into the United Steelworkers of America.

(See also: "Little Steel" Strike; Steel Industry Strikes.)

UNITED TEXTILE WORKERS OF AMERICA

This union was organized in Washington, D.C. in 1901 as an outgrowth of locals affiliated with the American Federation of Labor (AFL) and an independent union called the American Federation of Textile Operatives. It became a charter member of the Congress of Industrial Organizations and helped to organize the Textile Workers' Organizing Committee (TWOC) in 1937.

In 1938 the union split. Part of the membership returned to the AFL; the rest remained with the TWOC which later changed its name to Textile Workers Union of America. It is now affiliated with the AFL-CIO.

V ●●

VOLUNTARISM

The concept of voluntarism in the labor movement referred to the need for workers who sought improvements in pay or working conditions to rely on their own strength by joining the trade union movement. This gave them ability to use strikes, boycotts, and various other tactics to win the demands which they made through collective bargaining. Voluntarism was considered preferable to government intervention.

Voluntarism was the hallmark of Samuel Gompers and the American Federation of Labor. This philosophy was the natural outgrowth of labor's experience during the nineteenth century when government seemed to be pitted against unions and their objectives. Therefore, since government appeared to be hostile, the labor organizations had to build up their own strength.

This concept changed over the years to the point where unions now request favorable legislation and accept government intervention, in some cases even seeking it.

 W ···

WAGNER-PEYSER ACT

This law, adopted by Congress in 1933, provided for the creation of the U.S. Employment Service in the Department of Labor. In 1939 the service was transferred to the Federal Security Agency.

The Wagner-Peyser Act established a joint federal-state administration of the public employment services to be financed by matching federal and state funds, the federal payments to be based on population. A system of national employment offices was to be established wherever no public offices existed and assistance would be given in maintaining offices already functioning. The states were required to observe federal regulations and standards regarding operation of the employment offices, as well as certain policies for handling applicants.

In 1969 the U.S. Employment Service was abolished by reorganization of the Manpower Administration and its functions were assigned to the U.S. Training and Employment Service.

WALSH-HEALEY ACT

The Public Contract Act, also known as the Walsh-Healey Act, was adopted by Congress in 1936 and is administered by the Wage and Hour Division of the U.S. Department of Labor. The act provides that government contractors must pay their workers no less than the prevailing minimum wage scales for comparable work, observe the forty-hour week with an eight-hour day, employ no boys under sixteen or girls under eighteen years of age, hire no convict labor, and eliminate all unhealthful working conditions.

WESTERN FEDERATION OF MINERS

In 1892, after introduction of the machine drill, the mines in Coeur d'Alene, Idaho, were closed, their owners stating that they would reopen only if the miners would agree to a wage reduction of a dollar a day. The arrival of strikebreakers and government intervention followed, then so typical of the west. These events caused a strong reaction among miners from Montana south to Arizona, and in May, 1893, "Big Bill" Haywood and other labor leaders met in Butte, Montana, with some forty delegates from mining camps to organize the Western Federation of Miners (WFM).

The WFM affiliated with the American Federation of Labor (AFL) in 1896 but withdrew when the AFL failed to provide strike assistance. The history of the WFM was a series of strikes, violence, explosions, wars with sheriffs, deputies, armed guards, and militia. Haywood and the other leaders realized that their union could not stand alone, and since the AFL was a distant Eastern organiza-

205

tion dedicated to craft unions, the WFM formed the Western Labor Union in 1898. When worried AFL officials tried to woo back the WFM into the federation in 1901, the Western Labor Union became the American Labor Union to emphasize the national character of the organization, but neither of these federations was successful in attracting many unions.

In 1904 the WFM invited labor leaders and others interested in the movement to a meeting to consider building a new labor organization. The group decided that the solution would be to establish "one great industrial union embracing all industries—providing for craft autonomy locally, industrial autonomy nationally, and working class autonomy generally." The conferees decided to call a convention in June, 1905, and at that time the Industrial Workers of the World (IWW) was established.

The next year the WFM withdrew from the IWW because its leadership felt that the revolutionary nature of the IWW did not help its cause. After the WFM engaged the Butte Miners' Union in an interunion conflict during 1913–1914, its membership dwindled. The name was changed to the International Union of Mine, Mill and Smelter Workers which merged into the United Steelworkers of America in 1967.

(See also: William D. Haywood; Industrial Workers of the World.)

WILDCAT STRIKE

A wildcat strike is a work stoppage or strike which is conducted by the union members without the authorization of the regular union procedure for calling a strike.

WOMEN, PROTECTIVE LEGISLATION

The three broad areas in which legislation has been enacted to protect the best interests of working women are pay, hours of work, and working conditions.

The federal government took little notice of women until 1918 when the Women's Bureau was established within the Department of Labor. Its purpose is to improve the welfare of working women by studying the various problems which concern them. The three principal problems which the Bureau studies are opportunities for employment, working conditions, and better utilization of womanpower. Primarily a promotional and service agency, its expertise and knowledge are available through technical assistance, consultative, advisory, and information services. The Bureau has no enforcement power but makes recommendations regarding the many subjects which come before it for study.

Hours of Work. In 1847 New Hampshire limited the number of hours women might work and thereafter several other states adopted similar laws. The first enforceable eight-hour statute was enacted in Illinois in 1893. Ten years later Oregon passed a law providing that "no female shall be employed in any mechanical establishment, or factory, or laundry, in this State more than ten hours during any one day." In 1905 a Mrs. E. Gotcher was forced to work more than ten hours in Curt Muller's Grand Laundry in Portland. A fine of $10 was imposed and the matter was then appealed up to the state supreme court and thence to the U.S. Supreme Court.

Here, in *Muller v. Oregon,* the court held that a state had the right to set a maximum number of working hours for women. The state had hired the famous attorney, Louis D. Brandeis, to present its case. He based most of

207

his argument on more than a hundred pages of data gathered for him by social workers. The evidence showed how long hours of work impaired the health, safety and morals of working women. This decision handed down in 1908 proved a landmark.* Between the time the court acted and the start of World War I in 1917, forty-one states tightened their maximum hour laws for women or enacted new legislation.

Pay. Laws establishing minimum wages for women were slow in coming because labor unions and federations gave the matter little support. The California State Federation even opposed minimum wages, claiming that such scales might become maximum wages. Leadership in pushing for pay improvements finally came from social workers and others who were concerned about the shocking, low pay scales in the needle and textile trades. Twelve states passed laws setting minimum wages between 1912 and 1917. Although some states failed to enforce the new statutes, or court injunctions made them ineffective, additional encouragement to the movement came in 1917 when the U.S. Supreme Court in *Stetler v. O'Hara* declared Oregon's minimum wage laws constitutional.

Unexpectedly, the court reversed itself in 1923 in *Adkins v. Children's Hospital* when it declared unconstitutional a law which provided for minimum wages in the District of Columbia. The court said that it could not reconcile wage restrictions with freedom to make contracts. This cast a shadow over all the state minimum-wage laws

---

* Only three years before in *Lochner v. New York* the Supreme Court had declared a state law which limited working hours in bakeries unconstitutional because it violated rights of property and freedom of contract guaranteed by the Fourteenth Amendment. Undoubtedly Mr. Brandeis' compelling arguments were responsible for this complete change in thinking.

and was not resolved until 1937, at which time the court acknowledged that the liberty to make contracts was a fiction under existing conditions of employment. This decision in *West Coast Hotel v. Parrish* reaffirmed the right of states to adopt almost any reasonable form of wage and hour legislation.

By the 1960's twenty-two states had adopted equal pay laws which varied in coverage and effectiveness, but the problem of equal pay for equal work received scant attention from the federal government until 1963. That year Congress passed the Equal Pay Act which prohibited wage differentials based on sex after June 10, 1964, for all workers covered by the Fair Labor Standards Act.

Working Conditions. There is little evidence that the issue of safety in factories, which was of importance in the nineteenth century, focused on women. It might have been forgotten for some time had it not been for the Triangle Shirtwaist Factory Fire of 1911 which showed the need for reviewing the old factory and safety laws, formulating safety regulations, and punishing violators. Since that time, legislation has been passed to grant certain concessions to women in industry, but for the most part, women have had to share the same working conditions as men.

(See also: Louis D. Brandeis; Discrimination in Hiring; Triangle Shirtwaist Factory Fire.)

WOMEN'S TRADE UNION LEAGUE
A number of social workers and trade unionists met in Boston's Faneuil Hall in 1903 and formed the Women's Trade Union League (WTUL). They hoped to solve some of the problems working women faced, such as the need for special protective legislation and opportunity to join a union. The American Federation of Labor was not

then, nor later, interested in opening its ranks to women. Membership in the WTUL was extended to both men and women. In fact, anyone sympathetic with the League's goals was invited to join.

The League's purpose was to "aid women workers in their effort to organize; to assist already organized women workers to secure better conditions; to start clubs and lunchrooms for women working in big factories; to give and arrange entertainments for them; to notify secretaries of labor organizations whenever an organization was to be formed so as to avoid conflicts in regard to jurisdiction." Activities of the League included organizing, picketing, raising bail, working for remedial legislation, and publicizing the need to improve working conditions.

Numerous well-known women, including Jane Addams of Chicago's Hull House, Lillian D. Wald of New York City's Henry Street Settlement, and Mrs. Eleanor Roosevelt were active in the organization. Women of independent means rallied to assist the League and many attornies volunteered their services. In the Shirtwaist Makers strike of 1909, seventy-five wealthy members, including Anne Morgan, daughter of the financier J. P. Morgan, went on picket duty. They became known as the "Mink Brigade" and submitted willingly to arrest.

Shortly after World War I, the members of the WTUL decided to disseminate their ideas and program worldwide and, therefore, helped sponsor a congress for trade-union women. Delegates from several Latin American countries and twelve other nations, including China, met with representatives of the WTUL in Washington, D.C. Before they adjourned, they established the International Congress of Working Women and voted to set up an International Labor Office at the League of Nations. The International Congress also became affiliated with the

International Federation of Trade Unions which had been founded in 1901, was reorganized in 1919, and closed its doors in 1945.

The WTUL disbanded in 1947 since its officers felt that it had served its original purpose. The New York League was probably the most active of the dozen branches established in major cities of the United States. Rose Schneiderman, cap maker and dedicated trade unionist, became its president in 1943. She was one of those responsible for establishing the Bryn Mawr Summer School for Working Women which operated from 1921–1939. The New York League finally closed its doors in 1955.

WORKINGMEN'S PARTIES

During the early 1800's, as the home industries and small shops staffed with craftsmen gave way to the new merchant-capitalist system, workingmen gradually lost status in the public estimation. Now that he had voting privileges, the average laboring man felt that he must somehow assert himself politically as well as recapture the respect which previously had been accorded craftsmen and journeymen.

Craftsmen, mechanics, and laborers formed "workingmen's parties" in many parts of the country and developed Workingmen's Platforms which advocated all or some of the following reforms: universal male suffrage; a ten-hour work day; abolition of imprisonment for debt; abolition of chartered monopolies; free education for all; protection for one's wages through a mechanic's lien law; abolition of the militia system which permitted the wealthy to avoid service.

One of the first workingmen's parties was the Republican Political Association of the Workingmen of the City of Philadelphia which was formed in 1828 by the Mechanics' Union. The party had some success in electing local candidates but disappeared in 1831. Another such group was the Committee of Fifty established in New York City.

The workingmen's parties were short-lived and by the end of the Jacksonian period (1836) most of them had dissolved. In a sense they achieved their objectives because both of the major parties were now aware of the political importance of the workingman. The politicians sought the laboring man's vote and listened to his voice.

(See also: Committee of Fifty; Equal Rights Movement.)

WORKMEN'S COMPENSATION

Workmen's compensation is a form of insurance which provides financial assistance to commercial and industrial workers who have been hurt while on their jobs. The insurance gives medical help and pay to injured employees and death benefits and pensions to their dependents when death occurs.

Maryland passed the first state compensation law in 1902 but it, like several similar acts, was declared unconstitutional by the Supreme Court because it was held illegal to require employers to comply. As a result, many of the early laws were elective. The Federal Employees' Compensation Act of 1916 covered certain federal civilian workers and helped encourage most of the states to enact compulsory laws between that year and 1930. By this time there no longer was any question about the constitutionality of such laws, as the courts upheld workmen's compensation acts which required employers to comply.

In most states workmen's compensation is paid for entirely by employers who purchase insurance policies from private companies. In a few states workers also make small contributions. The insurance covers occupational diseases as well as injuries. Payments are made whether or not there is carelessness on the part of the employee or employer negligence. If a worker cannot continue in the same occupation because of injuries, most states require that job retraining be provided.

WORLD FEDERATION OF TRADE UNIONS

Delegates from fifty-six countries met in Paris in September, 1945, to establish a World Federation of Trade Unions. (WFTU). Shortly after its formation, the Russian members, as well as French and Italian Communists, tried to take control and convert it into an international Communist organization.

In 1948 the British Trade Union Congress and the Congress of Industrial Organizations (CIO) decided to break relations with the WFTU. The American Federation of Labor (AFL) cooperated, and as a result, in December 1949, representatives from fifty countries met in London and established the International Confederation of Free Trade Unions. Both the AFL and CIO were among the charter members.

One of the major activities of the new group has been to foster trade union education and encourage organization of unions in the less developed countries.

Y

Yellow-Dog Contracts

A yellow-dog contract was a written or oral agreement made between an employer and employee which provided that the employee would not join a union, or if presently a member, would resign. This form of contract was imposed by managements to prevent a union from organizing its workers.

The Norris-La Guardia Act specifically declared that yellow-dog contracts "shall not be enforceable in any court of the United States and shall not afford any basis for the granting of legal or equitable relief by any such court . . ."

(See also: Iron-Clad Oaths.)

SUGGESTED READINGS

Readers interested in current articles, pamphlets, or books or information on any of the subjects mentioned in this book are urged to consult the following reference tools:

The card catalog of your public, school, or university library.

The Readers' Guide to Periodical Literature.

The subject volumes of the current issue of *Books in Print.*

The New York Times Index.

Vertical File Index.

Public Affairs Index.

The annual supplements of leading encyclopedias.

The U.S. Department of Labor publishes a subject listing of its publications, *Publications of the U.S. Department of Labor,* which is available free of charge. The current issue at the time this book went to press covered the period 1965 through June, 1971. For a copy, or for current information about labor matters, write the Office of Information, U.S. Department of Labor, Fourteenth Street and Constitution Avenue NW, Washington, DC 20210. The telephone number is 202-961-2024.

The following entries which are marked by an asterisk (*) denote that the book is available in a paperback edition.

AMERICAN FEDERATION OF LABOR
Carroll, Mollie R. *Labor & Politics.* New York: Arno Press, 1969.
Gompers, Samuel. *Labor and the Employer.* 1913; reprint ed., New York: Arno Press, 1971.
Lorwin, Lewis L. *American Federation of Labor.* 1933; reprint ed., New York: Augustus M. Kelley, 1969.
Taft, Philip. *A.F. of L. from Death of Gompers to the Merger.* 1959; reprint ed., New York: Octagon Books, 1969.

APPRENTICESHIP
Beveridge, A. *Apprenticeship Now.* New York: Chapman & Hall, 1963.
Krush, Harry. *Apprenticeship in America.* Rev. ed. New York: W. W. Norton & Co., 1965.
Marshall, F. Ray & Briggs, Vernon M., Jr. *The Negro and Apprenticeship.* Baltimore: Johns Hopkins Press, 1967.
——*Equal Apprenticeship Opportunities: The Nature of the Issue and the New York Experience.* Ann Arbor: University of Michigan Institute of Labor and Industrial Relations, 1968.*

ARBITRATION
Elkouri, Frank & Elkouri, Edna A. *How Arbitration Works.* Washington, D.C.: Bureau of National Affairs, 1960.

AUTOMATION
Rusinoff, S. E. *Automation in Practice.* Chicago: American Technical Society.
Siberman, Charles & *Fortune* Editors. *Myths of Automation.* New York: Harper & Row, 1966.*
Woodbury, David O. *Let Erma Do It: The Full Story of Automation.* New York: Harcourt Brace Jovanovich, Inc., 1956.

BRANDEIS, LOUIS
Mason, Alpheus T. *Brandeis: A Free Man's Life.* New York: Viking Press, 1956.
Todd, Alden L. *Justice on Trial: The Case of Louis D. Brandeis.* Chicago: University of Chicago Press, 1968.*

CHILD LABOR
Clopper, Edward N. *Child Labor on City Streets.* 1912; reprint ed., New York: Garrett Press, 1970.

Markham, Edwin, et. al. *Children in Bondage.* 1914; reprint ed., New York: Arno Press, 1969.

CIVIL SERVICE

Arco Editorial Board. *Civil Service Handbook.* New York: Arco Publishing Co., 1965.*

DuPre, Flint O. *Your Career in Federal Civil Service.* New York: Harper & Row, 1967.

Krislov, Samuel. *The Negro in Federal Employment: The Quest for Equal Opportunity.* Minneapolis: University of Minnesota Press, 1967.

CLEVELAND, GROVER

Nevins, Allan. *Grover Cleveland: A Study in Courage.* New York: Dodd, Mead & Co., 1933.

Tugwell, Rexford G. *Grover Cleveland.* New York: Macmillan Company, 1968.

COAL INDUSTRY—STRIKES

Coleman, McAlister. *Men and Coal.* 1943; reprint ed., New York: Arno Press, 1969.

Roy, Andrew. *A History of the Coal Miners of the United States: From the Development of Mines to the Close of the Anthracite Strike of 1902.* 1905; reprint ed., Westport, Conn.: Greenwood Press Inc., 1971.

Sheppard, Muriel E. *Cloud by Day: A Story of Coal, Coke and People.* Chapel Hill, N.C.: University of North Carolina Press, 1947.

COLLECTIVE BARGAINING

Collective Bargaining Today. Washington, D.C., Bureau of National Affairs, 1970.

Marting, Elizabeth, ed. *Understanding Collective Bargaining.* New York: Macmillan Company, 1958.

CONGRESS OF INDUSTRIAL ORGANIZATIONS

Preis, Art. *Labor's Giant Step: Twenty Years of the CIO.* New York: Pathfinder Press, Inc.

DEBS, EUGENE V.

Cannon, James P. *E. V. Debs: The Socialist Movement of His Time, Its Meaning for Today.* New York: Pathfinder Press, Inc.*

Ginger, Ray. *Eugene V. Debs: A Biography.* New York: Macmillan Company, 1962.*

DEPRESSION OF THE THIRTIES

Bird, Caroline. *The Invisible Scar.* New York: David McKay Co., 1966.

Galbraith, John Kenneth. *The Great Crash: 1929.* Boston: Houghton Mifflin, 1961.

Suggested Readings

Paradis, Adrian A. *The Hungry Years*. Philadelphia: Chilton Book Co., 1967.

Shannon, D. A., ed. *The Great Depression*. Englewood Cliffs, N.J.: Prentice-Hall, 1960.*

DISCRIMINATION IN HIRING

Ferman, Louis A., et. al., eds. *Negroes & Jobs: A Book of Readings*. Ann Arbor: University of Michigan Press, 1968.*

Marshall, Ray. *The Negro and Organized Labor*. Somerset, N.J.: John Wiley & Sons, Inc., 1965.

Ross, Arthur M. & Hill, Herbert, eds. *Employment, Race, and Poverty*. New York: Harcourt Brace Jovanovich, Inc., 1967.

DRAFT RIOTS—1863

McCague, James. *Second Rebellion: The Story of the New York City Draft Riots*. New York: Dial Press, Inc., 1968.

EIGHT HOUR DAY

Gunton, George. *Wealth and Progress*. Freeport, N.Y.: Books for Libraries, Inc., 1887.

FACTORY SYSTEM

Kydd, Samuel. *History of the Factory Movement*. 1857; reprint ed., New York: Augustus M. Kelley.

FEATHERBEDDING

Leiter, Robert D. *Featherbedding and Job Security*. New York: Twayne Publishers, 1964.

Weinstein, Paul A. *Featherbedding and Technological Change*. Indianapolis: D. C. Heath & Co., 1965.

GOMPERS, SAMUEL

Mandel, Bernard. *Samuel Gompers*. Kent, Ohio: Kent State University Press, 1963.

Reed, Louis S. *Labor Philosophy of Samuel Gompers*. Port Washington, N.Y.: Kennikat Press, 1930.

Thorne, Florence C. *Samuel Gompers, American Statesman*. Westport, Conn.: Greenwood Press, Inc., 1957.

GUARANTEED ANNUAL WAGE

Becker, Joseph M. *Guaranteed Income for the Unemployed: The Story of S.U.B.* Baltimore: Johns Hopkins Press, 1968.

HAYMARKET RIOT

Harris, Frank. *Bomb: The Haymarket Riot*. Chicago: University of Chicago Press, 1963.

Snyder, Wendy. *Haymarket*. Cambridge: M.I.T. Press, 1970.

HAYWOOD, WILLIAM DUDLEY

Haywood, William D. *Autobiography of Big Bill Haywood*. New York: International Publishers Co., 1966.*

HOFFA, JAMES RIDDLE
Hoffa, James R. *Trials of Jimmy Hoffa*. Chicago: Henry Regnery Co., 1970.
James, Ralph & James, Estelle. *Hoffa and the Teamsters: A Story of Trade Union Power*. New York: Van Nostrand Reinhold Co., 1965.

HOMESTEAD STRIKE
Burgoyne, Arthur C. *Homestead*. 1893; reprint ed., New York: Augustus M. Kelley, 1969.

INDUSTRIAL REVOLUTION
Bucher, Carl. *Industrial Revolution*. New York: Burt Franklin, 1967.
Doty, C. S. *Industrial Revolution*. New York: Holt, Rinehart & Winston, 1969.
Hobsbawm, Eric J. *Age of Revolution, 1789–1848*. New York: New American Library.*

INDUSTRIAL WORKERS OF THE WORLD
Dubofsky, Melvyn. *We Shall Be All: A History of the Industrial Workers of the World*. Westminster, Md.: Quadrangle Books, 1969.
Renshaw, Patrick. *Wobblies: The Story of Syndicalism in the United States*. Garden City: Doubleday & Co., 1967.

INFLATION
Hazlitt, Henry. *What You Should Know About Inflation*. New York: Van Nostrand Reinhold Co., 1965.
Milton, Arthur. *Inflation: Everyone's Problem*. New York: Citadel Press, 1968.
Palyi, Melchior. *Inflation Primer*. Chicago: Henry Regnery Co., 1961.

INTERNATIONAL LABOR ORGANIZATION
Alcock, Antony. *History of the International Labor Organization*. New York: Octagon Books, 1971.

KOHLER STRIKE
Petro, Sylvester. *Kohler Strike*. Belmont, Mass.: Western Islands, 1965.*

LEWIS, JOHN L.
Alinsky, Saul D. *John L. Lewis: An Unauthorized Biography*. New York: Random House, 1970.*
Flanders, A. R. *Experiment in Industrial Democracy: A Study of the John Lewis Partnership*. New York: Fernhill House, Ltd., 1968.

LOWELL GIRLS
Scoresby, William. *American Factories and Their Female Operatives*. 1845; reprint ed., New York: Burt Franklin, 1967.

Suggested Readings

LUDLOW MASSACRE
Stein, Leon & Taft, Philip, eds. *Massacre at Ludlow.* New York: Arno Press, 1971 (from reprints of 1914–1915).

MIGRANT LABOR
Coles, Robert. *Uprooted Children: The Early Life of Migrant Farm Workers.* New York: Harper & Row, 1971.*

McWilliams, Carey. *Ill Fares the Land: Migrants and Migratory Labor in the United States.* New York: Barnes & Noble, 1967.

Wright, Dale. *They Harvest Despair.* Boston: Beacon Press, 1965.

MITCHELL, JOHN
Gluck, Elsie. *John Mitchell, Miner.* New York: Augustus M. Kelley, 1971.

MOLLY MAGUIRES
Broehl, Wayne G., Jr. *Molly Maguires.* Cambridge: Harvard University Press, 1964.

Dewees, F. P. *Molly Maguires: The Origin, Growth and Character of the Organization.* 1877; reprint ed., New York: Augustus M. Kelley, 1970.

MUCKRAKERS
Lyon, Peter. *Success Story: The Life and Times of S. S. McClure.* Deland, Fla.: Everett/Edwards, Inc., 1963.

NATIONAL INDUSTRIAL RECOVERY ACT *see* NEW DEAL

NEW DEAL
Freidel, Frank B., ed. *New Deal and the American People.* Englewood Cliffs, N.J.: Prentice-Hall, 1964.*

Fusfeld, Daniel R. *Economic Thought of Franklin D. Roosevelt and the Origins of the New Deal.* New York: Columbia University Press, 1956.

Hawley, Ellis W. *New Deal and the Problem of Monopoly.* Princeton, N.J.: Princeton University Press, 1966.

Moley, Raymond. *First New Deal.* New York: Harcourt Brace Jovanovich, 1966.

PENSIONS
Holzman, Robert S. *Guide to Pension and Profit Sharing Plans.* Lynbrook, N.Y.: Farnsworth Publishing Co., 1969.

Pelch, Michael & Wood, Victor. *New Trends in Pensions.* New York: Fernhill House, Ltd., 1964.

PINKERTON AGENCY
Horan, James D. *Pinkertons: The Detective Dynasty That Made History.* New York: Crown Publishers, Inc., 1968.

PULLMAN STRIKE
Lindsey, Almont. *Pullman Strike.* Chicago: University of Chicago Press, 1943.*

U.S. Strike Commission. *Report on the Chicago Strike of June–July 1894.* 1895; reprint ed., New York: Augustus M. Kelley, 1968.

RAILROAD STRIKES

Eggert, Gerald G. *Railroad Labor Disputes: The Beginnings of Federal Strike Policy.* Ann Arbor: University of Michigan Press, 1967.

Martin, Edward W. *History of the Great Riots.* 1877; reprint ed., New York: Augustus M. Kelley, 1969.

REUTHER, WALTER

Gould, Jean. *Walter Reuther.* New York: Dodd, Mead & Co., 1971.

Hansen, Beatrice. *Political Biography of Walter Reuther.* New York: Pathfinder Press, Inc.*

SHAW, LEMUEL

Levy, Leonard W. *Law of the Commonwealth and Chief Justice Shaw.* New York: Augustus M. Kelley, 1957.

SOCIAL SECURITY

Schottland, Charles A. *Social Security Program in the United States.* New York: Hawthorn Books, 1963.

SOCIALIST PARTY

Cannon, James P. *E. V. Debs: The Socialist Movement of His Time, Its Meaning for Today.* New York: Pathfinder Press, Inc.*

Seidler, Murray B. *Norman Thomas: Respectable Rebel.* Syracuse, N.Y.: Syracuse University Press, 1967.

Shannon, David A. *Socialist Party of America: A History.* Westminster, Md.: Quadrangle Books, 1967.

STEEL INDUSTRY—STRIKES

McDonald, David. *Union Man.* New York: E. P. Dutton & Co., 1969.

TEAMSTERS' UNION

DeArmond, Fred. *Managers vs Teamsters.* Springfield, Mo.: Mycroft Press, 1959.

Gamel, Donald. *Evolution of the Western Teamsters.* Berkeley: University of California Press, 1971.

TRIANGLE SHIRTWAIST FIRE

Stein, Leon. *Triangle Fire.* Philadelphia: J. B. Lippincott Co., 1967.

UNEMPLOYMENT

Dunlop, John T. *Program to Employ the Disadvantaged.* Englewood Cliffs, N.J.: Prentice-Hall, 1970.*

Fishman, Leo & Fishman, Betty. *Employment, Unemployment, &*

Suggested Readings

Economic Growth (Problem text for introductory courses in economics). New York: Crowell Collier & Macmillan, Inc., 1969.*

Johnson, Lawrence A. *Employing the Hard Core Unemployed.* New York: American Management Association, 1969.*

Komarovsky, Mirra. *Unemployed Man and His Family: The Effect of Unemployment Upon the Status of the Men in Fifty-Nine Families.* 1940; reprint ed., New York: Arno Press, 1971.

Woodriff, Ray. *Great American Resource: Unemployment.* New York: Vantage Press, 1970.

UNEMPLOYMENT INSURANCE

Becker, Joseph M., ed. *In Aid of the Unemployed.* Baltimore: Johns Hopkins Press, 1965.

UNITED AUTOMOBILE WORKERS

Pflug, Warner W. *UAW in Pictures.* Detroit: Wayne State University Press, 1971.*

UNITED BROTHERHOOD OF CARPENTERS & JOINERS OF AMERICA

Horowitz, M. A. *Structure and Government of the Carpenter's Union.* Somerset, N.J.: John Wiley & Sons, Inc., 1962.*

UNITED MINE WORKERS OF AMERICA

Brophy, John. *Miner's Life: An Autobiography.* Madison: University of Wisconsin Press, 1964.

Evans, Chris. *History of the United Mine Workers of America.* 1920; reprint ed., New York: Burt Franklin, 1971.

Hume, A. Britton. *Death and the Miner: Rebellion and Murder in the UMW.* New York: Grossman Publishers, Inc., 1971.

UNITED STEELWORKERS OF AMERICA *see* STEEL INDUSTRY—STRIKES

WOMEN IN INDUSTRY

Abbott, Edith. *Women in Industry: A Study in American Economic History.* 1913; reprint ed., New York: Arno Press, 1969.

Baker, Elizabeth. *Protective Labor Legislation with Special Reference to Women in the State of New York.* New York: AMS Press, Inc., 1925.

Henry, Alice. *Women and the Labor Movement.* 1923; reprint ed., New York: Arno Press, 1971.

Pinchbeck, Ivy. *Women Workers and the Industrial Revolution, 1750–1850.* New York: Augustus M. Kelley.

WOMEN—PROTECTIVE LEGISLATION

Brandeis, Louis D. & Goldmark, Josephine. *Women in Industry.* 1907; reprint ed., New York: Arno Press, 1969.

WOMEN'S TRADE UNION LEAGUE

Boone, Gladys. *Women's Trade Union League in Great Britain and the United States of America.* New York: AMS Press, Inc., 1942.

Suggested Readings

WORKINGMEN'S PARTIES

Hugins, Walter. *Jacksonian Democracy and the Working Class: A Study of the New York Workingmen's Movement, 1829–1837.* Stanford, Cal.: Stanford University Press, 1967.*

INDEX

Index

Index

Index

Index

Roosevelt, Eleanor, 210
Roosevelt, Franklin D., 6, 12, 39, 89, 123, 138, 139, 143-144, 149, 150, 174, 187, 192
Roosevelt, Theodore, 31, 38, 134, 200
Roper, Dan, 52
Runway shop, 170

Sabotage, 170
Sailor's Union of the Pacific Coast, 171-172
San Francisco General Strike, 172
Scab, 170-171
Schechter Poultry Corporation v. United States, 139
Schneiderman, Rose, 211
"Scranton Declaration," 3
Seamen's Act, 171-172
Seamen's Defense Committee, 53
Select Committee on Improper Activities in the Labor-Management Field, see McClellan Committee
Selective strike, 166
Seventy Years of Life and Labor, 171
Shanker, Albert, 26
Shaw, Lemuel, 173
Sherman Anti-Trust Act, 13, 164
Sinclair, Upton, 134
Sit-down strikes, 167, 173-174, 198
Skidmore, Thomas, 43-44
Slowdown, 186
Smith-Connally Act, 12, 122
Social Democratic Party of America, 23, 54, 176
Social Democratic Workingmen's Party of the United States, 175
Social Security Act of 1935, 150, 174-175, 193-194
Social Security System, 146, 174-175
Socialist Labor Party, 55, 175-176
Socialist Party of America, 53, 54, 55, 60, 86, 176-177
Socialist Trade and Labor Alliance, 55
South Carolina State Development Board, 169
Southern Illinois Coal Company, 87

Southwestern Railway System, 162-163
Sovereign, James R., 112
Soviet Russia, 128
Speedup, 186
Starr, Ellen Gates, 148
Steel industry strikes, 91-93, 124-125, 177-181
Steel Workers Organizing Campaign, 135
Steel Workers Organizing Committee, 124-125, 136
Steinbeck, John, 130
Stephens, Uriah S., 110-111
Stetler v. O'Hara, 208
Steward, Ira, 63
Strasser, Adolph, 78
Stretchout, 186
Strikebreaker, 181-182
Strikes
  Coal, 36-41; Cripple Creek, 85-86; Homestead, 91-93; Kohler, 113-114; Lawrence Textile, 119-121; "Little Steel," 124-125; Paterson Silk, 145; Pullman, 163-164; Railway, 161-165; San Francisco general, 172; Seattle general, 172; Sit-down, 173-174; Steel, 91-93, 124-125, 177-181; Textile, 186-187
Sunrise to sunset system, 62
Sweatshop, 182
John Swinton's Paper, 85
Sylvis, William H., 142

Taft Hartley Act, 13, 28, 36, 66, 103, 114, 119, 122, 129, 139, 140, 180-181, 183-184, 198
Tammany Hall (NYC), 67
Tarbell, Ida, 134
Taylor Act, 26
Teamster Conference, 90
Teamsters' Union, 198
Ten-hour day, 62-63
Ten-hour laws, 63
Textile strike of 1934, 186-187
Textile Workers Organizing Committee, 89, 203
Thirty-hour week, 188
Thomas, Norman, 166, 176-177
Thornhill v. Alabama, 12

232

Index

As a writer, businessman, vocational specialist, and researcher, Adrian A. Paradis has published widely in the last fifteen years, with thirty-five books in print or preparation, and innumerable articles to his credit. He has covered subjects that range from banking to biographies of contemporary businessmen and scientists; from public relations to religion; from vocational guidance to reference works; and from economics to law. In addition, he has worked on reports and special studies in his capacity as a corporate executive.

Mr. Paradis entered Dartmouth College in 1930 and later studied library science at Columbia University. When the Second World War broke out, he joined American Airlines, starting an economics research library for that company. He served for many years as Assistant Secretary for American before taking early retirement in 1968 to devote full time to writing. This aviation background is evident in his previous work, *Two Hundred Million Miles a Day*.

Mr. Paradis and his wife Grace, the parents of three children, live in Vermont. In addition to writing, they direct the New England Writing Associates, located in Woodstock.